Strategic Rest

Learn a new work style
free of stress, tension, and anxiety

Strategic Rest: Learn a new work style free of stress, tension, and anxiety (Second Edition)

ISBN 978-0-9889360-3-4 (e-book)
ISBN 978-0-9889360-4-1 (perfect)

Table of Contents

THE JOURNEY TO REST

"Christopher, you look exhausted. Are you getting any sleep?"

I was shocked by this executive's direct honesty, as he passed me in the hall after a meeting. And I was immediately defensive. Jim's genuine concern and authentic humanity caught me off guard. But I knew he was right – I was visibly tired after several weeks on the road. And I did not have a healthy set of habits to sustain the pace of constant travel and demanding projects. But I thought I had hidden the exhaustion and stress from my clients.

As a consultant to corporations and government agencies, I have travelled from city to city, month after month, for the last two decades. From one project to the next, my work life has required near constant movement, a never-ending series of airports and meetings. I did not sleep well on the road, and my job kept me on a revolving circuit of tough situations with clients and projects. I wanted to please them all, which was literally impossible, so I always felt just on the brink of failure. The flip-flop dynamic of barely-averted crises, followed by public success every few months, was grueling to me.

After a while, I tried to compensate with more caffeine. Several friends suggested meditation and natural supplements to reduce stress and help me rest. Those did help some, but my inner life was still full of potholes and blind curves. I felt frustrated and angry every time a client was disappointed with our team. Even after I'd had a good night's sleep, conflict, stress, and tension still simmered just below the surface.

Privately, I was afraid my inner drive and strong personality would not be enough to sustain my stressful lifestyle and work environment. Any plan for deep rest was so far down my "to do list" and took so long to achieve, I rarely enjoyed it. I spent the first half of every vacation unwinding, and the second half dreading my return to this demanding work environment.

Since rest never came easily, I just plowed on, determined not to become a victim of Corporate America and the materialistic ladder of success. I did recognize that my, "I eat stress for breakfast," hubris was a chronic problem – a weakness that I had to overcome. Impatience and a critical spirit were creeping into my family relationships and seeping into my social life. As I approached middle age, I was gaining weight, ignoring my real Calling in life, and suffering phantom stabbing pains in my abdomen that doctors could not diagnose.

I needed to learn to rest, not only physically, but mentally and emotionally. Deeply. I needed to heal, to experience a lifestyle of rest. Not just for a few more hours of sleep each night, but as a new way of life that could pave safer paths thru the deeper parts of my soul.

And that is when Jim stopped me in the hallway outside his office. He professionally but lovingly confronted me in my weakness. He recognized that I was struggling – that I had untapped potential that would never emerge until I dismantled my dysfunctional drive for performance-based approval, and learned to rest more comfortably, even as I worked hard to help my clients. In the days of soul-searching that followed that gentle confrontation, I realized that my greatest source of stress was not really my job itself. It was a nagging lie deep within my own soul – a lie that I would need to firmly grasp, and then yank out by the roots, before I could experience a healthy, sustainable lifestyle of work and rest.

I am a seeker, a questioner at heart. So, as soon as I noticed this loose thread in my psyche, I tugged at it a little. A few bad mental habits unraveled easily, and some resistance to the idea of rest gave way. That felt good, so I kept going. I kept searching, questioning. *Maybe... I began to hope, maybe I am not as broken as I feared. Maybe all my bravado and chutzpah and drive to be a top performer have together formed some false idol of achievement. Maybe, I wondered, if I slowly, carefully dismantle this self-defense structure I have built to keep clients and friends at arm's length, so their rejection does not hurt as badly... maybe this kind and strong and generous person that I hope still lives deep inside can finally and safely emerge, and begin to open up new depths of honest relationships. And one of my deepest hopes was to be able to finally, once and for all, crush my approval addiction, so that I could experience real and deep and sustained rest, and find the healthy pace and flow in a fulfilling, creative life that I had hoped for as a young man.*

My early experiments in rest and self-care worked, but only temporarily. Here is an example. As I cleared the security area in an airport early one morning, this was my self-talk:

"I am the happiest person around. I can't see anyone happier than me anywhere in this airport terminal. And if I do spot 'em, I will amp it up and out happy them, too. Folks, you are witnessing a highly competitive Type-A choleric learning to be present and content in the moment... Stand back. There may be some debris."

I toyed with these new ideas, testing them. I experimented in how I could not only survive, but truly thrive with a healthy heart and mind, without having to abandon a fast-paced, interesting career where I now had some fairly decent credentials. I liked my job; maybe I could learn to be healthy here?

Then about a year and a half ago, I got really serious about rest. I decided to focus on it as a major theme on a daily basis for a whole year. I dove into popular books, practiced meditation more consistently, and carved out more time for sleep at home and on the road.

A couple months later, I journaled again, en route to a meeting where I would have to defend some questions about project scope and timelines:

"Another day trip to hot sunny SoCal. Another day wrangling clients in meetings. Another decision that today I will be the happiest guy in the room everywhere I go. Because... I get to decide. And that ability to decide is a god-like power that I will not fail to exercise. And because... whatever I do over and over, gets easier each time."

That felt good, too. Again, the results were temporary, but I knew I was headed in roughly the right direction. The fear that my poor performance would cost me my job was replaced by hope that if I made a breakthrough here, in personal development, it could accelerate my career and open new possibilities. On a deeper level, I observed that my real voice began to emerge more often, stronger and more visible, no longer stuck and hiding.

I did not take time off to practice Strategic Rest. It boiled and broiled and stewed and simmered in the heat of my everyday life. Of managing six or eight projects simultaneously at work, with young children and a wife, and a life of writing and volunteering and starting a non-profit organization. I could not afford to stop earning a living while I did this deep work, to search out this mega shift that would pave the way for my next major career breakthrough. Even as I wrote and compiled these entries, our family made some huge transitions. I changed jobs, from a smaller local consulting firm to a national team of experts. Our fifth child was born. Our home was now too small, so we sold it to look for something larger out in the country. We did not find a farm, so instead we bought a motor home and travelled across the country... homeschooling our children from coast to coast, while I still worked full time every weekday and continued writing on the side. It has been a busy few years for our family. But that is the point of Strategic Rest: to find new ways to rest without waiting for the stars to align and the earth to stand still so that we can recoup.

After practicing Strategic Rest for a year or so, I finally learned to let go of chronic tension. I learned to keep breathing, steadily, peacefully, even while I worked long hours, week after week. I learned to keep rest as my primary focus, and trust that everything else will sort itself out. It became easier to let go and abandon plans that would never work. I learned to manage my own self-talk, and to process criticism and rejection. Those lessons and more are chronicled here, for you, in this book.

I am still a fast-paced, goal-oriented person. I still have more ideas than time, more hopes than days. I am still an undying optimist. And I am learning to hold all of that lightly. Because when work itself becomes both the means and the end, I am changed, and not for the better. I change from a lover of peace and people, to a slave to deadlines and a consumer of relationships. Rest does not replace work. It completely transforms work, infusing it with the life we really want to live.

And that has been my primary lesson: The Calling to live a life of Strategic Rest does not depend on my circumstances. I can make a deliberate choice to rest, right here, right now, in this present moment, with sweat on my brow. I have learned that rest is not at odds with a strong work ethic or professional and financial goals; it is vital to their fulfillment.

In some sense now, I feel I should go back to colleagues from the past decade or two and offer a deep and sincere apology. I was doing my best at the time, but I was focused on the wrong things. As a result, I often allowed unnecessary tension to build across relationships. I felt personally criticized or at risk when team members expressed what I now know is normal frustration over typical project issues. I often held back my deepest heart, taking the "safe" path of "professionalism," rather than building real relationships.

I finished writing this book a week after our consulting team delivered another million-dollar project. Throughout that entire assignment, under constant pressure, with tough deadlines, and in stressful conversations... not once had my approval addiction had its way. I had been working hard... fourteen-hour days for eleven weeks straight, so I took some time off. A few days later, I woke up mid-morning, later than normal. I rolled out of bed and heard my wife talking to someone in the living room. They laughed. We had visitors. Normally, my internal dialogue would begin shaming me for sleeping in so late, for appearing to be lazy to whoever was out there. I would kick myself for not having opened the front door to greet them, cup of coffee in hand, household chores done. But this morning, things were different. I felt completely relaxed and at ease. I was actually proud of myself for sleeping in. I was proud that I was prioritizing rest. I even wanted to show that off, a little bit. That is when it hit me: my values had shifted. My internal dialogue had changed. I no longer judged myself only on performance, but also on how well my heart and mind were able to adjust to healthy cycles of work... rest... work... rest... work... rest... Never just work, work, work; never just rest, rest, rest. Then, I had another epiphany. I remembered that it normally took me at least four or five days to decompress after a large project, even on vacation. In this case, it had taken only a few hours, from close of business on Friday to midday Saturday. Sure, I was still tired. I slept a lot for a week. It had been a long-haul project. But I was not carrying the normal residual stress, tension, or strain on relationships this time around. My creativity had not suffered. I had truly turned a corner in my personal and professional development. I had made a significant change.

I am still learning the skills and habits of Strategic Rest. But I can tell you this: it is so good to be free and breathing easy.

How to use this book

This book contains notes from my journey over the past few years, from chronic stress, to learning how to deliberately choose "rest" in any circumstance. These pages contain my observations, jotted down on airplanes and in hotels, as I stepped out of a client conference or into a taxi. They are insights into my own soul that I offer to you, just in case you have struggled with similar demands for work, and an inner life that has been unable to find sustained rest, for whatever reason. I can tell you: there is hope.

Strategic Rest is far more than just a pill and a long nap. It is not about how to take a better break, but rather how to break those thought patterns that push you to overcommit, overwork, and over-stress. In speaking with hundreds of colleagues about Strategic Rest, I have concluded that years of long hours and chronic stress are not badges of honorable service. They are bandages that hide worn and weary souls that have been searching for That One Thing that will finally validate their existence, so they can finally rest.

But your job performance will never really satisfy that need in you; you can always do more, and better. No, what you are really hoping for, working so hard towards, is proof of your intrinsic value as separate from your performance. And your endless frenetic activity – however noble or justified your cause – will never help you answer that question or fill that need… to know that you are worthwhile, just as you are. You need time to heal and rest, to reconnect with your true heart, apart from your day-to-day performance. There is no job in the world better served by your chronic tension and emotional strain, than with a whole heart and fresh creativity. Strategic Rest might be the best thing that has ever happened to your career. It has been for me.

These lessons on rest have been the most expensive of my work life. But I offer them here for you in the pages that follow. These are simply my reflections. Notes from the trenches of a high-pressure job, which has been, for me, the fault line between rest and fear.

Some readers enjoy these notes as poetry, as a source of inspiration.

Others have read them, one each day, for a ninety-day focus on rest.

Above all, I hope they help you search your own heart to find deeper places of rest, to eliminate the fears behind your anxiety, tension, and stress.

Strategic Rest is about living deeply while we work. When we develop a lifestyle of rest, we create more room for things that matter most. We let go of unhealthy, unfruitful habits that hold us back from living life with our whole hearts. When we learn the skills of Strategic Rest, we carry our best job performance, deepest insights, and our healthiest leadership style with us into every meeting, conference, conversation, and project, day after day.

Be at peace, my friends. And work hard.

Part 1

LETTING GO

The idea of "letting go" of things at work may seem counterintuitive to many of us, especially those who serve as leaders in the workplace. Since I have accepted certain responsibilities, and am expected to carry that load, pull my weight for the team, and perform my job well... how much of that can I really let go of? Wouldn't that be irresponsible?

But letting go is not irresponsibility. Quite the opposite... letting go of unproductive tension, strain, and negativity – even letting go of outdated ideas or ineffective methods – is one of the most responsible things I can do as a leader. Responsibility is simply my ability to respond well to the world around me. Letting go is the vital leadership that precedes every visionary transformation.

The power to choose what I hold on to, and what I let go of, is fundamental to both productive work and Strategic Rest.

In this section, I will share some of the poetic reflections that have allowed me to grant myself the time to rest, to refuse to constantly carry improper or ill-fitting burdens, so that I could recover my true heart and clear mind.

Walk with me into this mental journey, this process of letting go of unproductive strain. Take your time. I encourage you to move through these pages slowly, feeling as much or more than you think. Because when we rest, we give our hearts a chance to re-emerge, and help lead our lives and careers with stronger instinct and truer direction.

Catch and release

Worry is mental atrophy. It is repetitive thoughts, circling the drain of self-pity and fear, an endless, exhausting, and unproductive loop.

Rest is the practice of capturing those thoughts, then releasing them – letting them go, and replacing them with the gracious truth.

Rest is the practice of releasing grace into the present moment.

— STRATEGIC REST —

Noticing is a key aspect of Strategic Rest... becoming mindful of your own emotional state and mental patterns, so that you avoid getting stuck on your own thoughts and let go of worries with intention.

So, what are you sensing just now? What thoughts are circling your mind repeatedly? Can you catch those momentarily, and release them, at the same time releasing grace into this moment, to replace mental noise with a sense of calm?

Stillness

Stillness displaces judgment. When you are still, you see as clearly as you can see, without the distortions of guilt or blame.

Stillness disables perfectionism. When you are still, you stop striving towards the impossible, and allow beauty, truth, life, and art to emerge.

Stillness defies rejection. When you are still, you trust your own evaluations above all others.

Stillness is the quietest war on the planet, destroying wasted effort without prejudice. It is the fastest path to peace and self-acceptance.

Stillness is both the means and the end.

– STRATEGIC REST –

Tension and overwork are bad habits.

It is impossible to change bad habits instantly.

Rather than trying to stop something "cold turkey," which often leads to inconsistency and frustration, set an appointment for yourself each day to practice calm rest for a few minutes. No matter what else is going on during that time – wherever you are, whatever you are doing – calm rest will be part of how you do that thing.

Increase the length of your daily practice of rest each week or so. If you find it a challenge to keep yourself at rest, or in a restful state of mind, for these longer periods, drop back a few minutes each day to something more achievable. But keep it up. Do not quit.

Eventually, your entire being will begin to prefer – even crave – your deliberate practice of calm rest. And within a few months, you will have made one of the most significant transformations in your life: the ability to easily and consistently let go of tension and overwork.

Be still, and know.

Three things

Reach for a pen and write on the palm of your hand three things you are worried about right now.

Now, sit quietly for a few minutes... just breathe... and relax... and mentally release each of them, one at a time.

Wait there, until you have let it go, then move on to the next.

Now, every time you see the words on your hand... let them all go again.

— STRATEGIC REST —

Write down three or four things that are dominating your thoughts or draining your energy today... then find a quiet place for about five or ten minutes and just go through the mental exercise of releasing each of them, one at a time. Release the tension, your desire to control the outcome, the worry and stress... then take a deep breath and move on to your next task.

Fill the vacuum

It is not enough to simply let go of tension. Nature abhors a vacuum – so if all you do is release stress as a mental exercise, then more tension and stress will soon return to fill the void they left behind. With that approach, to keep up with life, you would need to release that tension again and again every few minutes, like a ship in a storm whose pump runs constantly to keep water out of the hold.

So, when you release tension and stress, fill that that space with conscious thoughts of gratitude, goodness, and comfort. Reject negativity and then shift your focus to anything that brings you love, joy, peace, patience, kindness, goodness, and self-control.

It is a simple mental exercise to help you embrace the skills and habits of rest. And you deserve to rest.

– STRATEGIC REST –

Here is an exercise called The Three Tens. Grab paper and pen, and finish each of these three sentences with ten different statements, for a total of thirty positive declarations:

"Today, I am thankful for…"

"Today, I respect myself for…"

"Today, I will show love and compassion to myself and others because…"

As you practice this exercise, it becomes easier to move your thoughts to gratitude, respect, love, and compassion as you let go of tension and worry.

To see things new

The biggest obstacle to personal change is your bias that twists all new information to confirm what you already believe.

To see things new, for what they truly are, is the beginning of re-creation.

To see things new, you must let go of all your prior judgments, assumptions, and evaluations.

This is uncomfortable. You have collected those judgments, assumptions, and evaluations to protect you from pain. To release them even for a few moments feels risky. Can you trust that Truth will re-emerge, that it can survive without your help?

To see things new, you must risk... you must let go long enough to sit back and watch the situation reform itself in your mind, casting a new light, a new form, a new hope, a new possibility, a new texture on your prior beliefs, allowing you to see new options and methods you had missed only moments before.

– STRATEGIC REST –

Which pressing, demanding, risky situations are you facing now, for which you would like to have a new hope, a fresh perspective, and a path around?

Pick one, and ask yourself... what are your long-held assumptions, judgments, and evaluations for that situation? Can you let those go, for the sole purpose of allowing a new and broader understanding to emerge? Do it now. Completely. And with no deadline for the new perspective to emerge. Just release your prior judgments and biases and allow the situation to exist for a while without those. Favor detachment and observation over dependence and control.

Journal this experience, so you will gain wisdom when you look back years from now, to see how your willingness to let go opened up new possibilities.

(Breathe.)

Conscious breathing is the fastest way you can let go of tension and relax.
So, rest today, on purpose.
Your thoughts feed your emotions.
Your emotions fuel your thoughts.
The breath sits between them... necessary and neutral.
We cannot fail to breathe.
Sometimes, we get stuck on a thought.
Or a feeling.
But we cannot get stuck on a breath.
We must inhale, then exhale... letting go several times a minute.
The breath is a coach, teaching us not to hold on to anything.
Thoughts come, and they go.
Emotions come, and they go.
It is when we get stuck on a particular thought or feeling that we carry chronic tension.
By focusing on the breath, intentionally, for a few moments... we remind ourselves to allow our thoughts and feelings to naturally come and go.
We avoid getting stuck, and thus release tension, and carry less throughout the day.
So, breathe.
Allow yourself a few moments to just focus on the breath.
Allow your breath to remind you to let go of that which is used up, spent, and no longer helpful.
To release tension, worry, and anxiety.
Just... breathe.

– STRATEGIC REST –

Look at your calendar and pick a time... set an appointment for three minutes – a reminder to simply sit quietly, with no task or agenda, and focus on your breath. This is a deliberate exercise to inject a sense of rest and release into your busy workday. No special techniques. Nothing fancy or complicated.

Simply sit and breathe. Focus only on your breath. If your mind wanders, simply notice, and resume your focus on the breath.

When you are done, set another appointment to do this exercise again in a few hours.

Just... breathe.

When you stop

When you stop judging, you will feel love more deeply.
When you stop trying to control things, you will find new peace.
When you stop counting only what you can see, hope will find you.

— STRATEGIC REST —

Make a mental list of two or three important situations you would like to, or are trying to, control or measure or evaluate.

Now, take a moment to understand how much of your mental energy is wrapped up in those few situations. Sure, they may be important – that is fine. For now, simply notice all the energy you invest in them. Now, see if you can let go long enough for peace to replace worry, for hope to appear – without even having a plan, for love to extend itself towards those involved.

Practice and performance

You may be called to perform once, for every hundred or thousand times you practice.

Don't beat yourself up over one poor performance.

Focus instead on daily practice.

Practice rest when no one sees you.

Practice letting go of little stresses, criticism, and expectations.

Practice ignoring bad stuff and verbalizing good things.

Then, when you are called to perform – to rest through a stressful situation – give it all you have… not for them, but only to observe where you might need more practice.

Then go home and rest again. Let go of that one performance and get back to your practice of rest.

– STRATEGIC REST –

Make a list of any restful practices you would like to allow yourself to enjoy each day or week. Then, you will have some practical options as you follow any inclination to let go of your chronic tension and overwork and become more deeply peaceful and calm.

An invitation to rest

Peace is simply an invitation to rest during that time between your last major battle… and your next one.

Rest prepares you for your next victory.

So, now, it makes sense to rest.

— STRATEGIC REST —

"All of humanity's problems stem from man's inability to sit quietly in a room alone."

– Blaise Pascal, *Pensées*

Countdown to desperation

If you cannot find a way to rest in your present circumstances, then somewhere out there is a clock counting down the hours to your next moment of personal desperation.

To rest well in any situation, you must develop new skills, like letting go of stress and frustration, maintaining a healthy detachment, practicing meditation, teamwork, and getting enough sleep.

And of course, being present in the moment, rather than always living forward into some future possibility… or backward into some past experience.

– STRATEGIC REST –

What if your moments of desperation were completely optional?

What if you could decide, right now, not to participate in your next one?

Or the one after that?

What if the single deciding factor for whether you will have a moment of desperation at all is simply your willingness to let go of frustrations and unmet expectations now, so that you can come to perfect peace with things just as they are, right now?

Can you do that?

Right now?

Self-Love

Why do we avoid or devalue self-care?

Why do we starve ourselves of our own affection, and then wonder why we feel alone and desperate?

As young people, many of us are taught not to be self-ish or self-centered or self-absorbed, and rightly so. But have those directives polluted everything to do with caring for our selves? Self-rejection, self-judging, self-criticism, self-hatred; we engage in these self-oppressing "self-ish" behaviors far too frequently. But why only the negatives, and not also the self-affirming acts, such as self-love, self-compassion, self-kindness, self-respect, and self-love?

A wise teacher once said, "love others as you love yourself." Do you see the sequence built into that instruction? First, we love ourselves, to set a standard… to carve out depth, to create new space in our souls and fill it with grace. It is almost as if we must first develop the capacity and skill for love by practicing it first on ourselves, and then we can extend that grace and generosity to others with greater skill and determination.

If you were to love someone, as you now love yourself… how would they feel? Would they welcome that treatment, or would they distance themselves from you? And how would you feel, to be loved as you love them?

When is the last time you were simply enamored by your own goodness, kindness, acceptance, and forgiveness?

When is the last time you really felt the full emotional impact of your own love and respect?

Rest follows love. To rest more deeply, is to love our selves more willingly.

– STRATEGIC REST –

For the next hour or two, talk to yourself as you would talk to someone you deeply love.

The tradeoff

The discipline of letting go is a deliberate choice. It is not passivity. It is focus. It is a force multiplier: it magnifies and maximizes every other effort.

Letting go replaces a rigid, control-freak requirement that your plans must be followed exactly, with a far more intelligent and dynamic awareness that is called, "Trust."

Letting go is the first step to replacing your sheer strength of will, which is exhausting, with the greater and far more powerful instinct.

But letting go bears a high cost: you must trade your illusion of certainty for the possibility of an outcome that is better and different than you can envision right now from a position of scarcity and fear.

— STRATEGIC REST —

"Are you tired? Worn out? Burned out…? Come to me. Get away with me and you'll recover your life. I will show you how to take a real rest. Walk with me and work with me – watch how I do it. Learn the unforced rhythms of grace. I won't lay anything heavy or ill-fitting on you. Keep company with me and you'll learn to live freely and lightly."

– Rabbi Y'shua, according to Mattithyahu

Give it time

When it is cold and dark, and you cannot see to find your way home... do what we did in ancient days: eat and drink, hunker down, and sleep quietly until morning.

Morning will come in its own time, and each morning looks new.

Just give it time.

For now, rest.

— STRATEGIC REST —

"Everything will be okay in the end. If it's not okay, it's not the end."
– John Lennon

Beware the blue-faced people

When your soul breathes… it lets go of everything that is used up, old, and toxic, and accepts what is good, life-giving, and healthy.

Your soul breathes to exchange fear, failure, and shame, for strength, purpose, and another chance.

Those who cannot let go of stuff have zero capacity to change things for the better. They are stuck… they inhale, inhale, inhale, but never exhale. Eventually, they faint – give up, go passive, disappear – or explode.

Consciously choose to allow your soul to breathe, especially during times of tension or stress. This vital, natural exchange… letting go of what is useless and used up and taking in what is new and present and available… is the basis for forgiveness, friendship, and peace.

When the soul can breathe, it can rest.

Beware the blue-faced people.

– STRATEGIC REST –

An unpacking exercise: Just before bed, grab a notebook or loose paper and set a timer for fifteen minutes. Now, write about your deepest concern – the situation you have been unable to release – until you are calm. Destroy the papers you have written. Follow this plan for three nights in a row, then give yourself a break.

Part 2

TRUST

Most of us live so deeply within our daily grind and chronic weariness that we have completely forgotten what it is to feel rested, refreshed, and creative... to live at full strength.

Trust offers a cure for that: a new lifestyle of rest that fully supports your strong work ethic, recognizes your performance demands, and offers a simple set of practices for sustainable productivity and leadership.

Real trust is like a cool drink of water, a breath of fresh air, a safe and spacious land. It is the one place where you are free to drop your guard and relax. And it is large enough to allow for every change life brings.

Rest asks that you exercise all the trust you have at this moment, but then it returns that trust to you, stronger and deeper than it was before.

A new measure of strength

To carry constant stress is not a show of strength, but a lack of trust, and the result of poor training. Occasional pressure is normal. Chronic tension is not.

Any worthy accomplishment requires a certain measure of persistence.

Deep rest requires training in a different measure of strength: Trust.

– STRATEGIC REST –

To rest deeply is to "carry nothing" from moment to moment, from day to day. What does the encouragement to "carry nothing" mean to you?

Authenticity

"Too busy to rest," is a mathematical error.

You will get more done in less time, and be more creative and effective, when you are well rested and refreshed.

Want to get more done? Take a real break, then hit it again, hard.

There is great profit in rest.

More is seen, heard, felt, and understood from an unstressed state.

The authentic self is not the worried, exhausted, tense person.

To live life from a place of rest… is to serve the world with your whole heart.

— STRATEGIC REST —

Where do you hide when you are tired? Mentally, emotionally, and physically… how do you protect yourself from others when you do not feel rested and refreshed? Now, contrast that with memories of yourself at full strength, as you worked with your whole heart on something you felt strongly would help others.

Can you begin to recognize that difference as you work your way through this next few days? Notice when you begin to hide, notice when you re-emerge, and most importantly, notice those influences that invite you to hide, and those that inspire you to step more fully into your Calling.

Authenticity is a compass for emotional freedom.

To believe like a child

Acceptance without understanding.
Love without performance.
Trust without question.
There is a time to ask, to learn, and seek to understand.
But when the questions cannot be answered, and understanding is impossible...
there is only room for child-like acceptance.
That is a place to rest.

— STRATEGIC REST —

It is no admission of weakness to confess that some things are beyond your control, or defy your comprehension, or present an impossible choice.
It is not ignorance that embraces mystery – but wisdom.
Accepting your limitations frees you to search for help outside yourself, or even better, to rest patiently for the best possible outcome.
It is not all up to you.

Daily exercise

Waiting tests how easily you slip into rest, versus demand control.

Waiting in line at the market.

Waiting for a partner to make a decision.

Waiting for a child to finish a lesson.

Waiting drags you into the mental gym every single day, so you can exercise your trust muscles.

But waiting is not resting, is it?

Waiting requires that you maintain an expectation that things will change. You must monitor that expectation as you wait.

Resting makes no such demands.

When you rest, you accept things as they are, knowing that they will change at the right time.

And making that shift, in a moment, from waiting to resting, is the heart of our daily practice.

— STRATEGIC REST —

Here is a new exercise regimen.

For the next week, each time you find yourself waiting, use that time to practice rest. Power down… let go… and settle in. Focus on your breath, as you inhale and exhale normally. No need to change how you are breathing – simply observe each breath. If you would like to shift your focus periodically, try noticing areas of your body that are tense or tired, and focus on releasing the tension and relaxing those areas. If you would like to shift focus yet again, begin a mental list of things you are thankful for. Then, you can shift your attention right back to the breath again.

Above all, do not allow your mind to simply dwell on work or problems or negative possibilities. Give yourself permission to rest from all of that for a while. If it is really important, it will still be there after you rest.

These exercises of focused mindfulness have proven benefits for mental, emotional, and physical health, and they are like weightlifting for your ability to focus for extended periods of time. So, when you do return to work, you will be rested, refreshed, more creative, and better able to focus.

Control

You try to exert control where fear is at work.

If you find yourself looking for angles, ways to manipulate, or struggling to influence a situation… turn your attention instead to the deep-rooted fear in your heart and deal directly with that fear.

Then you can let go of your desire to control, and simply rest while the situation resolves itself.

– STRATEGIC REST –

"The less effort, the faster and more powerful you will be."
– Bruce Lee

The source

Do the birds, while it is still dark, call forth the morning sun?
Or does the sun, in its nascent gloom, awaken the birds to sing?
Describe for me your source of hope, your vision for a life yet unseen.
Is it you, that calls for new light... or does the light awaken you from your present darkness?
And how is it, that the light rarely calls to you, except from within the night?

— STRATEGIC REST —

Have you lately stood for a while in the presence of your source of hope?
Have you rested there, for a while, with no agenda, requests, or deadline?
Have you simply rested at the headwaters of all that is good in your life, observing the grace and power that you cannot fathom, touching it but unable to grasp it?
Have you?
When will you, again?

Act as if

To speak what should be, as if it already were…

to treat others as their best self, though they have not yet changed.

to see what is ahead, that is good and right and lovely, and embrace it with your whole heart.

to behave as though this challenging situation had already changed.

the relationship was already mended.

all debts were paid.

as if there was no reason for worry or fear.

These are all acts of willful rest.

To act as if… is to let faith and hope take you by the hand and lead you to a life of greater love.

To act as if… is to exercise even greater strength.

To act as if… is to survey new lands, draw new maps, and pave new roads to far greater personal peace and health.

To act as if… is to exercise your greatest personal liberty and freedom.

To act as if… you must release what was before.

– STRATEGIC REST –

The ability to see what could be, but is not yet… to make a strong, deliberate decision to change the world around you – this is personal leadership. From a position of rest, you can more easily recognize those things that are outside your control, let go of unrealistic expectations and useless negativity, and choose instead to focus on the single option that is always available to you: your ability to choose a new and different way of being.

Simple

Stop resisting goodness.

– Strategic Rest –

What benefit do you receive from worry?

From carrying fear?

From rehearsing problems, conflicts, or criticisms?

What if you just assumed that goodness surrounds you on all sides, and is always present with you and available, even when others cannot see it?

What if you lived with that assumption – willfully – for a whole day?

What if you simply allowed goodness to surround you on all sides, and then noticed the difference it makes in your day?

Safety

Love invites you to a quiet place, for a one-on-one conversation.

The safety and care you sense in that place will invite you to invest even more trust there.

Privately, Love says to you, "I will be your shield."

Rest… right there. Just take a breath and let that soak in.

– STRATEGIC REST –

In what areas of your life is trust a visitor, and not a permanent resident? Take a few minutes to sit quietly and allow trust to take root in each of those areas, one at a time. Be sure you protect – even defend – trust's right to live there. Allow it. Invite it. Welcome it.

Part 3

TRIMMING

Chronic and repeated failures make us reluctant to develop high trust relationships. That resistance to trust undermines teamwork and creates tension, and an inability to really rest, while you are working, and between heavy work periods.

The deliberate act of "trimming" is a quiet evaluation of what is effective, and what is destructive, in our daily lives. If we perform that evaluation from a position of tension or stress, we are likely to trim too much of the wrong things, and too little of the right things.

Strategic Rest connects you more deeply with your true heart, your life Calling, and the meaning inside the work you do every day. From this position, the act of trimming is an act of love – a series of choices to leave behind old, ineffective thought patterns and negativity in favor of generosity and health.

Deadwood

Yesterday's conflicts and failures are no longer productive.
They are deadwood and have served their purpose.
There is no benefit to rehearsing them repeatedly.
So, let old conflicts and failures go.
Prune the deadwood.
Cut away those thoughts that do not bear healthy fruit, so you can focus your energy on the present season's new growth.

– STRATEGIC REST –

Why not plan one weekend each quarter, four times a year to deeply rest and accomplish nothing? Just get away, to simply rest and recover. Do nothing. Exert as little energy as possible. Sit back, relax, recover, sleep, meditate, walk slowly or not at all.

At first, it seems to take effort to do nothing. That is psychological momentum… just like the feeling when you have been driving or riding fast for a while, and come to a stop, it feels like you are still moving. Your mind plays the same trick on you after long periods of work. Allow it, effortlessly. Don't resist it. Just let it be. It will change on its own. Focus on breathing and resting and simply putting out as little effort as possible.

This restful experience follows a process of stages, as momentum gives way to fatigue or even exhaustion. Then nervous energy may demand some form of entertainment. But no, sit quietly instead, simply allowing all to be as it is. More sleep. Eating, drinking, but no effort. Creative energy emerges next. Lists and plans and things you must not forget about… capture these on paper, so you can forget about them for a while. They are in a safe place now; pull them out when you get back to work and handle them responsibly then. For now, let them go. More ideas. New ideas. Good ideas… you could start planning, now, making notes and thinking through, problem solving.

But no, this is rest, not work. So, jot down a few words to remember later, then let those thoughts go. Because rest is important. Read books, but only those books that allow you to continue or even deepen your rest; nothing related to the projects or work ahead. Read to rest, not to educate yourself.

Time moves on. More sleep. Your mind finally calms and quiets. This is where you need to stay. Still and quiet, for a long period of time. Focus on the most basic necessities: breath, water, sleep, food, meditation, releasing and letting go anything that demands effort.

These extended sessions will teach you more about how you process work versus rest, but will also strengthen your basic skills in terms of rest, focus, letting go, and meditation, making it easier to enter into rest on a daily basis when you return to your regular work life.

Less is more

Perhaps what you need is less, not more.
Fewer things, not more.
Fewer options, not more.
One thing to focus on at a time, instead of several long lists or projects.
Simple trust, to replace your complex, worn out methods.

— STRATEGIC REST —

How can you simplify your day today?
What can you set aside?
When will you focus on only one thing for a while?

Capture your thoughts

A mind at rest is free to observe the present, without the distraction of a thousand incomplete tasks, regrets, and half-baked ideas.

To put your mind at ease, capture every thought...

Some are captured in an Idea Cloud, a list you keep of worthwhile works and untapped potential.

Some are captured in your diary or calendar, as a Next Action to be completed at the right time.

Some are captured to entertain you and be observed over time. These thoughts wish to tell you a story... from which you can learn wisdom, the source of predictable cause and effect.

Others are captured and found to be immature and incomplete, so they serve as an opportunity to discern Truth from Lie... a process that frees you from debilitating self-criticism.

A mind at rest is not a thoughtless mind, but a mind that thinks well.

– STRATEGIC REST –

How often do you intentionally capture, then release your thoughts?

Can you begin a new practice, to notice repetitive and worrisome thoughts, then write down a reminder for yourself to take action on the thought? Put an appointment on your calendar to deal with the situation at the right time, and then you are free to let go of the repetitive and worrisome thoughts, knowing that you will deal with it at the right time.

Now, you can simply be present, and enjoy this moment, in peace.

Death to critics

Negative criticism is an ego trip for the speaker, and a waste of time for you. The same is true of self-criticism. If a thought does not move you towards your Calling – you are free to ignore it.

Only one kind of critic is worth a hearing: the one who knows you, cares for you, understands your Calling and your current struggles, and offers their critique in a way that gives you hope, strength, and better clarity to help you reach your goals.

– STRATEGIC REST –

Sometimes, the best response to a critic is encouragement. Criticism is the child of fear and envy. In all likelihood, your worst critics worry they are in competition with you. They compare themselves to you and come up short. So, simply encourage them. Affirm them, and their work.

The selfless act of love is one of the most liberating obligations in all humanity.

"My philosophy is: It's none of my business what people say of me and think of me. I am what I am, and I do what I do. I expect nothing and accept everything. And it makes life so much easier."
– Sir Anthony Hopkins

Living under a threat

Unreasonable expectations.
Improper measurements.
Impending demise.
Misplaced blame.
Unfair criticism.

These are symptoms that your Calling is not aligned with the means or ends of those around you who expect, measure, blame, and criticize. Their scrutiny seems misplaced, their directives half foolish. Beneath it all is an underlying threat: If you misstep, there will be consequences.

You can toe the line for a while and go along to get along... in order to get what you need, as a means to your own end. But ultimately, if your means and ends differ significantly from those you serve, you will need to decide on a timeframe to leave and walk your own path.

The deeper caution, of course, appears when you see a series of these misaligned relationships over time. That could indicate several things:

- It could be that you are trying to serve your Calling well, but in the wrong place or time.
- It may be an indication that you misunderstand your own Calling; if you are unwilling to submit to it, to serve it with selfless sacrifice, then you may be one out of sync with the world around you, including those you serve.
- Or, it could be that you are simply living for now under a constant injustice, limited by others' selfish agendas. In this case, the question for you is simply a matter of patience and stewardship: Is this the right place for you to serve your Calling, for however long it takes to see the season change, and fruit to appear?

– STRATEGIC REST –

What specific and persistent threats have you been living under?
Which of those are internal, created by your own thoughts and expectations?
Which are external... suggested, assumed, or imposed by others?
Are the threats real? What would happen if you simply chose to ignore them?
What is the minimum level of effort you can invest in addressing threats, so that you can focus your full heart and mind on the valuable and generous work of your Calling?

Those who deal in shame

Demanding work often creates a culture of fear. And a culture of fear constructs a false framework designed to protect itself from the fallout of near certain failure. Perhaps there has been so little safety here, for so long, that no one believes it is possible to succeed. So then, the culture of fear begins to make false promises: "If you perform perfectly and can help us avoid failure, you will be accepted." But it never pays off, because all who live in the culture of fear prevent their own success through chronic defensiveness and a greater focus on what might go wrong than on creating high trust, highly productive teams.

Those who use fear and suspicion to get what they want, trade in the currency of shame, in the spirit of slavery.

Those who deal in kindness and truth, trade in the currency of grace, in the spirit of freedom.

Do not seek the approval of those who deal in shame, lest the courage of your own true heart abandon you.

The free soul cannot afford to deal in the currency of shame.

To dismiss the rejection of those who do not love the good that you love is an honorable act of integrity.

— STRATEGIC REST —

To either join the culture of fear or be kind and tell the truth from a whole heart that refuses the allure of false promises from the culture of fear. Today, you must choose to either accept your role as a victim of the dysfunction around you, or to transform it through loving honesty.

What is your choice?

Healing

Forgiveness is an honorable act of self-love.

To forgive is to suspend your self-protective judgment, deliberately creating space for an alternative meaning and final outcome. It is not denying the truth about what happened, but rather denying yourself the luxury of punishing them for what happened, based only on your limited understanding of those events. It is not justifying their actions, it is releasing the pain in your soul, so that love can live there, too... even if primarily for your own health and benefit, not theirs.

The energy required to remain vigilant against what originally caused you pain, the offense... is unnecessary now. You no longer have a reason to remain attached to the pain. You can release the pain without excusing the wrong. Let go of it, simply so that you can rest more easily.

To rest more deeply, forgive more deeply.

You still need to heal. But you can do that more easily when you are no longer attached to the pain or the offense.

— STRATEGIC REST —

Is it time, now, for you to begin healing? Can you love yourself well enough now, to allow yourself to forgive, for the sake of your own heart and health?

Breaking out of shame

"Life shrinks or expands in proportion to one's courage."
– Anais Nin

Shame is an ongoing offense, not just a one-time event. It is the consistent message that says, "You have never been good enough. You will never be good enough. There is something wrong with you, at the core, that makes you less than enough and undeserving of the goodness you desire."

To break out of a system of shame, a culture of fear, requires courage and resilience and persistence.

You must look up at the stars and set your own course towards freedom and love and goodness, regardless of where others around you are going.

You must also forgive, consistently, as a daily practice, because the natural by-product of a culture of shame and fear is resentment.

You must begin to process every shaming, controlling, fear mongering remark you hear differently than you have in the past.

You must choose to reject the lies.

Distance yourself from the fountain of lies.

And replace the lies, with truth and love.

– STRATEGIC REST –

Are you willing to chart this course, to walk the long path from shame to love?

What new thoughts must you embrace to contradict the old messages of shame and fear that have echoed through your mind for years?

Can you identify the fountain of those lies... then define what "distance" means to you?

Life is difficult

Life is difficult.

Even when you are healthy and know how to rest... life is difficult.

Getting free of the need for certainty and control is necessary, but it does not free you from the fact that... life is difficult.

As you learn to rest well, you will move from surviving to coping, coping to living, and living to giving. Your joy goes deeper. You learn to practice self-love. Your relationships improve. You practice self-care.

And... life is still difficult.

— STRATEGIC REST —

"Life is difficult. This is a great truth, one of the greatest truths. It is a great truth because once we truly see this truth, we transcend it. Once we truly know that life is difficult – once we truly understand and accept it – then life is no longer difficult. Because once it is accepted, the fact that life is difficult no longer matters."

– M. Scott Peck, *The Road Less Traveled*

Part 4

ABANDON TO GOODNESS

When I began to test the interplay of rest and work, it became clear to me that these two are siblings, not opposites. As I began to practice *Strategic Rest* on the job, at a client's site, in a tense meeting... I noticed that I had a choice – an opportunity to rest well, then and there, and when I did, it enhanced my work performance.

That observation drove me to look more deeply into some definitions and assumptions I had about a style or approach to work that creates stress, versus restful practices that bring more peace to intense, demanding periods of work.

One of the distinctions that emerged was the difference between hope and fear, as an underlying ethos or motive for tasks at work. Hope is defined as the expectation of something good and helpful... and fear as the expectation of something negative or painful.

Ebb and flow

Watch the waves on the beach… see how the ebb precedes the flow?
The last wave draws back before the next one drives forward.
The longer the last wave's ebb, the more powerful the next wave's flow.
Do not resist rest – the ebb. Do not be anxious about a "drawing back." Instead, accept it, knowing that the time will come soon for you to push forward again with a new and stronger flow, crashing thru old barriers with unparalleled new power.
Rest is not stasis.
It is thoughtful preparation before a meaningful breakthrough.

– STRATEGIC REST –

Is your work life in the midst of an ebb, or a flow?
Does it seem that things are pulling back, or pressing forward faster than you can follow?
And given that reality, what is your healthiest mindset, just now?
Is it trust and deep rest in preparation for what is next?
Or is it trust and hard work to participate in the soon coming breakthrough?

The river

Sure, you could sweat every single boulder, every rapid, and every whitewater. You could strain against the current, worry in angst about what is around the next turn. You might stop and ask the advice of others who have paddled this stretch before you.

Or, you might relax a little more… simply choose to rest in the knowledge that the river itself is taking you someplace, and the only way you will miss that… is if you quit.

Sometimes, it pays to conserve energy and just let the current carry you there. You cannot ignore immediate obstacles. You do have to keep your head above water. But those are small, easy adjustments. You do not need to fight the whole way, sweating, straining to make progress.

Let the river carry you. Let the current do its own work. Minimize your movements. Catch your breath. Enjoy the ride. Relax. Trust in the River of Life to take you where you need to go.

– STRATEGIC REST –

Do you believe in the River? Or have you concluded that life is all up to you?

How would your experience in stressful situations be different if you put complete faith in this "current," trusting that it is taking you where you need to go?

Mystery

We do not easily tolerate mystery. To tolerate mystery requires us to accept that some things are outside our control.

Because we are so interested in controlling things, we are driven to understand how everything works, and why things happen. So, when something big happens, we feel compelled to figure it out. We try to invent some kind of meaning for every event in our lives. But we are likely to get that meaning wrong, because we cannot yet see the full picture. And getting it wrong prevents us from truly learning and healing... because learning and healing require Truth.

Tolerance for mystery is not the end of logic, but the beginning of understanding. When we can rest in a place of mystery, we will develop deeper questions and new perspectives.

What if it is not for you to see the 'why' behind a significant event in your life, or to label each event as good or bad? If you can accept mystery, and wait for meaning to be revealed, you gain new space right now to learn and to heal. The alternative is to risk casting a premature judgment, as you impose an incomplete "That was good!" or "This is horrible!" meaning on something you may not yet be prepared to grasp, and you could never really control.

Quick judgments are rarely wise judgments.

Here is the mystery: some of your deepest pain and suffering is the soil in which your Calling will fully develop.

— STRATEGIC REST —

Which large mysteries have you chosen to ignore?

Can you entertain them now, as the questions that will lead you to deeper goodness than your intellect alone has ever known?

Can you rest in the knowledge that the entire purpose of mystery is to raise questions you would not otherwise know to ask? And the answers to those questions could change the course of your entire life.

Not yet

There is a reason it hasn't happened.
You just do not know why.
It may be the wrong place.
The wrong person.
The wrong scenario.
But… there is a reason.
So, for now, you are free to either wait, or rest.
Waiting is harder – it bears an expectation that something will change.
Resting is easier – it bears no expectation at all, but accepts what is, now.
To rest is to allow life to author the next page, without knowing whether the present chapter is near the end, or a new chapter is about to begin.

– STRATEGIC REST –

Can you replace incessant analysis with deep trust?
Can you cease to wait, and rest instead?
Can you enjoy life as a co-author of your story?

Uncertainty

Certainty is a farce… a saccharine substitute for one of the essential proteins of life: hope.

Certainty is a false counterpoint to life's natural rhythm of peaks and troughs that carry you toward your Calling.

To embrace uncertainty is to look Life fully in the face and declare with a loud if shaky voice:

"I am right here. Your enormity of joy and sadness could crush me if it came all at once… but moment-by-moment, you temper my soul into the hardened steel with which I will build my dearest memories and greatest triumphs. I am not afraid of vulnerability or uncertainty. I am terrified of living without trust, with a dead heart. So, bring it on… let's do this."

– STRATEGIC REST –

When is the last time you felt your own hope, at its fullest strength?

Quiet competition

Can you be the happiest person in the room, everywhere you go today?
The happiest person in the meeting?
At the market?
On the road?
Not just a shallow, trite, empty smile.
Not faking or denial.
But an intentional practice of peaceful joy.
Can you choose true, deep, restful joy?
Try it.
Practice quiet joy.
Decide to be the happiest person in the room, everywhere you go today.

– STRATEGIC REST –

Is joy a cause or effect?
Is it a decision or a response?
Can you practice the act of deep joy, as a deliberate choice?
Try it now and observe your own thoughts as they fall into line, respecting your decision.

Risk

You know the risks on this path.
You have been here before.
But now… review those risks again, using only your heart.
You will find that your heart is more courageous than your head.
You must honor your heart's inexplicable strength, and let it lead you into your Calling, with kindness and grace.

— STRATEGIC REST —

"No bird soars in a calm."

– Wilbur Wright

Self-preservation

It is right to say: "Not right now," when you are wounded, to buy yourself more time to heal.

It is wise to refuse to swim with sharks while you are bleeding.

If you are wounded, weak, or tired, you deserve time to rest and heal before you enter the water again.

That is not a luxury. It is basic safety.

But then, once you are rested and healed… God save the sharks!

– STRATEGIC REST –

In what situations are you most likely to sacrifice your physical or emotional health in favor of "important" work?

And, in those situations, would it be possible to:

1. Team up with others to share the work?

2. Trade off tasks, responsibilities, or deadlines to spread the work?

3. Say no to the work?

Giving up

When you feel completely overwhelmed, just go ahead and give up. It is not the same as quitting. Giving up completely feels great, and any real, legitimate problems will boomerang for sure, so you will get another shot at them soon. Just go ahead and let go of all your judgments, priorities, and urgency for a bit.

Give up, just for a few minutes. Completely.

How much of your stress is simply the echoes of demands long past, versus legitimate issues that need your attention this week?

Put your current stress to a test, to see whether it is real or only imagined.

— STRATEGIC REST —

"By letting it go it all gets done. The world is won by those who let it go. But when we try and try, the world is beyond the winning."
– Lao Tzu

Reflection

Before heading to work, we consider our visible reflection in a mirror.
But do we also consider the reflection of our hearts and minds?
Now, what do you really want, as part of your daily inner life?

– STRATEGIC REST –

"If we would give, just once, the same amount of reflection to what we want out of life that we give to the question of what to do with a two weeks' vacation, we would be startled at our false standards and the aimless procession of our busy days."

– Dorothy Canfield Fisher

Part 5

TRANSFORMATION

"Too often I would hear men boast of the miles covered that day, rarely of what they had seen."   — Louis L'Amour

Within the first few months of our lives as infants, we develop our earliest bias: either the world is a safe place where our needs will be met and we will be nurtured, or it is not, and we must struggle with feeling alone and unheard.

For many of us, the healing nature of personal transformation is the act of reconsidering this initial bias, and coming to terms with the fact that, while life is difficult, we do not need to remain alone and unheard; we can give and receive love and develop deep trust.

The implications to our work life here are enormous; work may be viewed as a place of conflict and strain, or as an opportunity for us to express our best lessons, as value to the clients, customers, and colleagues we serve.

The source of all personal transformation is not academic education; it is deeper and is often the direct result of increased attention to self-care, self-love, and self-challenges.

The spirit of poverty

The spirit of poverty tries to convince you that work versus rest is a daily dilemma. "You cannot have both," it lies to you. Because the spirit of poverty consistently pressures you into lopsided and unfair tradeoffs: work versus rest, safety versus love, meaningful work versus financial security. So, the fruits of a spirit of poverty are desperation, tension, and worry, while the fruits of a spirit of abundance are generosity, contentment, and peace.

All of nature follows a steady rhythm of work and rest: waves, seasons, days and nights, the sun and moon and stars. When you embrace rest as a strategic tool, you align yourself with this natural, normal, life-sustaining cadence. Your greatest accomplishments in life are shaped and formed through endless cycles of work and rest, and by your deliberate choices to live life in a spirit of abundance. A spirit of abundance will fuel your creativity, inspire new theories and ideas, and gently eclipse what is old and useless with what is new and fruitful.

The spirit of abundance is a set of heart-habits that helps you shed unproductive thoughts and enter a zone of personal peace and safety that you can carry into every meeting, every conversation, and every task.

But how do you get there? How do you move from a spirit of poverty, on the path towards unfair dilemmas and regrets, to a spirit of abundance, where rest and work are equal partners, like day and night?

Real transformation takes time. You can make some small changes on a whim, temporarily. But under pressure, you are likely to quickly fall back on your most deeply ingrained habits: the old survival patterns that wear you out and strain your relationships. So, you need real transformation. You need to learn to really, deeply rest again – even in the midst of the daily grind. You need to develop a new lifestyle, a new mindset, and a new set of habits.

Rejecting a spirit of poverty is not just a single decision – it is a thousand individual choices, hour by hour, day after day. You must be re-trained.

The transformation that allows you to abandon a spirit of poverty and embrace a spirit of abundance consists of a thousand individual choices that all orbit one single brilliant sun: Gratitude. Gratitude is the daily practice that focuses your thoughts – not on what you had and lost or want but do not yet have – but instead on all that you have been given that is good, and most especially that good which is present with you now.

– STRATEGIC REST –

Practice a total focus on gratitude for a solid hour today. During that hour, choose to reject any idea of lack or want or unmet hope or expectation, and deliberately focus your thoughts on gratitude for the good near you now.

The rudder

The most powerful, persistent thoughts in your mind create the life that you live. Not because your thoughts control others, but because they control you. Your most powerful, persistent beliefs influence every decision, every word, and every action. They are so deep within you that you are no longer consciously aware of them – they have become part of who you are. They automatically chart a course for you in every relationship, in every creative effort, and in the formation of your character. They create a bias that causes you to notice or overlook certain things.

Without your conscious awareness, some of those deep ideas may be slowly sacrificing your health on the altar of work and stress and busy-ness.

You can reverse that flow. Take the time to quiet your mind. Create a safe place for a few minutes each day for your heart to re-emerge and speak kindly to you. Let it speak Life and Truth. Then, make those new statements you hear the focus of your thoughts for the rest of the day.

Think life. Speak life. Quiet yourself and listen to the voice of Life Itself, deep inside you.

To change the course of your life, you must change your deepest thoughts.

Rest lets the quiet voice of Truth be heard.

– STRATEGIC REST –

How have you been misunderstood lately?

Sit quietly and allow your heart to share with you it's real motives – what you know to be true, and what you really intended... not what was misunderstood or miscommunicated.

Do not be distracted by the result or outcome of the misunderstanding. Instead allow yourself to focus on the purity of your original intentions, and to appreciate that for a few minutes, just as it exists still in its purest form.

Now, stay there for a while, and allow yourself to feel the love and respect that develops naturally as you observe the good and kind and generous nature you intended to convey.

Finally, let go of the negative outcome, the misunderstanding, and instead simply continue to focus on the purity of your intentions.

There is no vengeance here, only continued kindness, and the confidence that Truth knows you better than anyone else.

It is your greatest ally.

Emerging

Strategic Rest clears a path in your soul for the emergence of new ideas, new energy, and new habits. The breakthrough you have been hoping for may now depend solely on your deep work to release the old and allow the new to emerge. Those seeds in you... the wisdom, hope, and passion that lie just beneath the surface... are waiting to feel the prolonged warmth of the sun again, to be drenched over and over in the rain of rest. Then when the time is right, they will emerge for all to see.

And so, simply allow the sun, allow the rain. Meaning: Continue your practice of prolonged periods of rest, allowing joy and self-love to be the predominant energy in your heart and mind. This deep personal transformation is the key to your next harvest, to your next breakthrough personally and professionally.

– STRATEGIC REST –

If your concept of rest is simply that you stop work, then you will miss most of the benefits of rest. If your concept of "letting go" is that you simply come to a standstill, stop movement or involvement, then when you resume work, you will remain basically unchanged. You step right back into stress-filled old patterns that suck the life right out of your soul.

The whole purpose of rest is to create a safe place that allows you to experience unconditional love and acceptance. That is the end game for rest, the purpose for coming to a quiet place. It is not just accepting things as they are and coming to peace with them... it is accepting yourself as you are, learning to love and appreciate yourself deeply, and coming to peace with the goodness that lies at the core of who you really are.

Your public performance may vary, but in the quiet place of Strategic Rest, motives matter most, far more than any other place.

The purpose of letting go is to prove to yourself that you are worthy of love, just as you are, because at your core you are pure and lovely and strong and helpful and holy and sacred and commendable.

And none of that has anything to do with your work.

Never has. Never will.

Getting used to peace

Many of us have lived from time to time with prolonged interpersonal conflict, as children, and now as adults. So, we often find ourselves unable to settle into periods of prolonged peace. We find it difficult to really unwind, relax, and enter into deep, sustained rest. We feel as if we are waiting for the other shoe to drop. Our radar swings round and round every waking moment, hypersensitive to detect the next threat as soon as it arises.

This is normal for anyone who has suffered trauma or abuse – or sustained "do or die" tension and stress in the workplace.

But that is old, outdated thinking. There are no enemies here, only friends. The enemies only still exist as echoes in your heart and mind. This present quiet is your opportunity to distinguish yourself again, as separate from those old conflicts.

What does it look like, a warrior in a time of peace?

– STRATEGIC REST –

How much energy do you expend each day, subconsciously scanning for threats?

This is a natural practice for any warrior, to defend their community and protect the territory.

But in a time of peace, absent any real conflict, that subconscious awareness – the low-level but consistent vigilance – can be redirected to constructive purposes. A warrior in a time of peace lives to serve, to hold a position within their community that stands for all that is good and just and right. Their awareness is meaningful as they look for opportunities to step in and affirm or support, or directly assist if needed. Their Calling is to protect and defend, and that Calling is demonstrated differently in peace and battle.

Same Calling; different season; different expression.

Alignment

The difference between the straw that breaks the camel's back, and the breakthrough that leads you to peace, is not your circumstances, but your response.

The difference between your *breaking* and your *breakthrough* often comes down to your decision to let go of the demand to have everything your way, the way you have had things before, the way you – in your very limited experience – believe things should be.

If you cannot let go, the strain of controlling everything will eventually break you, or your relationships, or both. You were not meant to control your environment – that load does not match the shape of the Calling you were meant to carry. It is poor alignment between the burden and the bearer.

Proper alignment only comes with trust. If you can let go of the need to control, every divergence from your ideas and plans will help to grow your trust... to save you... to strengthen you... to heal you from fears rooted in the mishaps and pain of your past.

Your redemption is freedom from old, invalid fears.

Rest is not a lack of exertion; it is coming into proper alignment with the present moment, so that everything is as easy as possible.

You were meant to travel the world, not govern its weather.

– STRATEGIC REST –

"In the end, only three things matter: how much I loved, how gently I lived, and how gracefully I let go of things not meant for me."
– Buddha

The garden of the mind

If you lack the creative energy to pursue your Calling… you may be wasting energy fighting back the weeds that grow from lies hidden deep in your heart and mind. Wouldn't you rest easier by observing those lies, digging them up, and replacing them with Truth?

Every thought is a seed.

Every seed becomes a plant.

Every plant bears fruit.

Consider the sweetest realities of your life. At their root is Truth that has set you free to live and love as you were always meant to live and love. Between that deep-rooted Truth and your enjoyment, you will find a thriving garden of positive thoughts.

Observe the weeds in your mind that choke out your creativity and waste your energy. From which thoughts did those weeds grow? At the root of each is a Great Lie. The Lie must die for the weeds to become powerless – for your garden to thrive and bear sweet fruit, with little effort.

The garden of the mind bears the fruit of the soul.

Tend it well.

Eradicate the lies.

Allow the Truth to bear sweet, easy fruit in you.

– STRATEGIC REST –

Take a few moments today to simply sit and observe nature.

Find something organic nearby, and simply notice it.

Try to watch the grass grow… literally.

No agenda. Just calm observation.

See the pattern of waves on the beach, or water in a pool or fountain.

See the clouds in the sky, as they are, shifting, reforming.

Consider that your soul exists within the same context as all the rest of nature… some thoughts and emotions constantly shift and reform. Others grow and form more slowly, but always following their DNA – their basic nature.

Who is the steward of your soul? Who tends to its health and well-being?

Basics

Breathe.
Work.
Look.
See.
Let go.
Breathe.
Listen.
Accept.
Breathe.
Work.
Let go.

— STRATEGIC REST —

**Focus on the fundamentals today: Just breathe.
Let go. Accept. Rest. Work.**

New habits

Healing is not always calm, quiet, and still.

Chaos, movement, and strenuous demands can test you, push you, and if accepted, can usher in new lessons and help you form new habits.

Restful habits, that teach you how to complete more work with less effort and remain calm and at peace even while surrounded by crisis.

The pressure and effort may become familiar or normal, but each day in that environment represents an opportunity to find new and easier ways to get more done in less time.

It is an opportunity to form new and more restful habits.

To correct misperceptions about your limitations.

To try out the practice of Strategic Rest while hard at work.

– STRATEGIC REST –

Define a new habit you would like to develop as you embrace Strategic Rest.
Write it down and place it where you will see it several times each day.
Some habits take years to develop; others take days.
There is no right answer.
Do what is restful for you.

Failure

It is impossible to be disqualified from your Calling.

It is impossible, because your Calling is not about you. It is timeless and bigger than you. You can neither define nor limit it. You did not choose it; it is offered to you by Life Itself. It exists – not as a demand or a mandate – but as an open invitation that defines you and directs you towards selfless service in a community.

Any notion of your qualifications or disqualifications is nothing more than distracting pride or a thinly veiled excuse. Your Calling knows nothing of those. You are Called. Period. It is one of your unchangeable attributes. Follow it, or do not follow it, but do not suggest failure as a valid reason to ignore it.

Your failure and success are irrelevant – mere experiments and purifying exercises.

Your Calling does not exist to fulfill you... you exist to fulfill your Calling.

So, people do not fail. Plans fail.

People either quit... or make a new plan.

– STRATEGIC REST –

List three of your most heart-wrenching failures.

Now, consider your best notion of your life Calling. This is very rarely clear to any of us, so simply accept whatever you believe to be your Calling as of this moment... your present understanding: How are you uniquely called to serve the world with selflessness and love and generosity – not from some future circumstance, but from your present circumstance?

Next... consider how your most painful failed efforts and plans may have given you a deeper understanding of those you are Called to serve, and how those experiences may have helped to mature your means and methods to serve them?

Think on these things now and allow yourself to move from shame to love for your own past, to a new place of appreciation and respect for failed plans and ridiculous mistakes.

Darkness to light

We each carry thru life our own personal Books of Meaning, where we have unconsciously recorded the historic causes of our pleasure and pain. We judge each new experience by what is already written in our books. We evaluate every interaction, not only on its own merit, but with the added meanings of prior interactions. "What did she really say? Was it good or bad? Helpful or hurtful? Does it belittle or support me? Embarrass or respect? Offend or validate?"

So, we hear a statement of praise, instead as a backhanded compliment.

We experience helpful insight, instead as patronizing conceit.

We perceive a story shared in good humor, intended to create a common bond, instead as part of an endless competition over who has traveled further, escaped worse calamity, or collected shinier coins.

They intend love, but our Books of Meaning wrap their words in a Lie, and their intended care is lost to us. Our previous pain places a burden on our relationships, draining each new experience of its pure joy and positive value. Our efforts to deepen friendships are plagued by a judgmental parasite that prevents us from building trust and enjoying deep intimacy.

There is a Great Lie hidden among the pages of every Book of Meaning. Here it is: "There is something wrong with me, something broken, and I must hide it. That is why I will never be fully known and loved as I really am."

This Great Lie is an active agent, common to every living human on the planet. It is the remnants of a cruel, destructive "kill or be killed" and "eat or be eaten" reality that no longer exists. But its essence lives on in us, and if we allow, it will pervert and pollute every potentially positive message we receive from friends and lovers, bosses and colleagues.

Moments of deep pain inscribe the largest and darkest marks in our Books of Meaning. To turn the tables on the Great Lie, we must write every new mark in the words of an even Greater Love: self-love and the love of truth, in big, bold, colorful, beautiful script that declares the purest of all Truths...

"I am loved, and I am worthy of love. I give and sacrifice and do well for others, with little regard for my own profit. I make mistakes, but grace lives there, too. And in spite of all the pain I have lived thru, my heart is still kind and good. I am still capable of loving and being loved, and Life invites me to do so. So, I will continue to risk... to give and receive love and grace. Because that is why I breathe."

We must love ourselves out of the Lie that we are worthless.

Deep personal change rarely comes from a miraculous mountaintop high, but more often from the quiet, determined formation of new internal habits, and the deliberate acceptance of truths yet unproven.

Here is your hope. You will not die in the dark.

Carry a blank page with you for the next two days. Jot a quick note of the time and place whenever you find yourself feeling inadequate to an assigned task, unworthy of a compliment, or tempted to hide rather than engaging others with openness and transparency.

After a day or two, sit quietly and look back over your notes with this question: "Where are the lies or half-truths that stirred me to hide, to shrink, or to dismiss myself from these situations?"

Now, observe the lies… can you begin to perceive them as separate from yourself? Can you detach from them? Can you begin to contain, then contradict, every lie or half-truth with candid honesty that honors your best efforts and good intentions?

Break up the pan

Farmers who plow the same field season after season know that over time, there develops a "plow pan" beneath the soil they till. This layer of compacted earth builds up over time, with each pass of the plow, until it becomes thick and impermeable. Water cannot pass thru to the soil beneath; roots cannot penetrate it and remain shallow and vulnerable to drought and heat. And the harvest – the end results of a full season's work – suffers.

The pressure and pace of each day's work has the same effect on our souls, building up layer after layer of tension and negativity.

Farmers periodically set their plow far deeper than normal, to dig up the plow pan, breaking through it to allow their crops full access to the cool moisture and rich nutrients below.

Strategic Rest allows you to break up deep layers of stress and anxiety, releasing concerns that are old and gone, or out of your immediate control, so that you can more readily access peace and health.

Periodic deep rest maximizes your efforts and produces your best results, season after season, harvest after harvest.

– STRATEGIC REST –

Can you list the chronic sources of the tension and negativity that you carry? Now, can you identify these areas of your heart and mind that have become calloused and self-protective, as a result of the ongoing strain?

Sit quietly with those for a moment. Observe them, with no intent to change them. Learn from them. Study them, with curious detachment. Stay there long enough – or go and come back, if you must – to allow your heart and mind to reveal new places for rest to dig deeply within your soul, to break up those hardened places, and allow healthy growth and new experiences.

Once it changes

One day you will awaken with a deep sense of calm, feeling rested and peaceful. All worries, concerns, and unfinished business will seem distant.

When this happens, throw out an anchor and stay there as long as you can. Your practice of rest is paying off. After living with emotional noise and tension for a long time, you have had a breakthrough.

Enjoy it. Sink deep into the calm. Bask in it. Minimize any negative that comes your way. You are actually rewiring neural pathways in your brain to accept and even gravitate towards this sense of peaceful well-being.

Why are we so timid about self-love? Self-love is not selfish, any more than self-feeding and self-exercise and self-hydration and self-education and self-leadership. It is not narcissism. It is not arrogance. Love is not a zero-sum game; loving yourself more does not take anything away from anyone else. Deep rest is part of self-care, which is really motivated by self-love.

Perhaps the limit to which we can ever experience the love of others... is set by the depth to which we experience our own self-love. Rest, there.

– STRATEGIC REST –

When is the last time you felt overwhelmed by your own love and respect: the rich warmth and deep reassurance and joyful confidence of someone who knows you intimately... who sees your pure motives poorly performed, your imperfect struggles to do what is right, your private successes hard won... and truly appreciates all of that, and respects you for it? What if a healthy, intentional focus on self-love is the fastest path to personal transformation – to becoming the healthy, strong, whole-hearted person you are meant to be?

Cynics

A cynic is nothing more than a wounded idealist, frustrated by a lack of progress, burned out by long hours without enough visible progress or restorative rest. A cynic does not actually doubt the vision. They still believe in it with their whole heart. But they are terrified that they are inadequate to that vision. After trying so hard, for so long, their own doubts about their prior failures turns into treasonous mockery of their Calling. Desperate for validation, a cynic begins to fuel the fires they built for comfort with their own brand of public negativity, as a desperate ploy to garner compassion and praise from others, for all they have invested and endured. So, criticism disables every new plan or idea before it is launched.

Bitterness and cynicism are the burnt, smoldering foundation of a Calling that failed due to your impatience and improper methods. There is supposed to be a beautiful building there — everyone knows that. It was to be vital, necessary, functional, and beneficial to the community. You can still see the outline and envision the form as it was intended. But frustration over the immensity of the task, the impossible odds, and the lack of visible progress allowed the warmth of the first fire on that grand new hearth to consume the entire structure before it was complete.

Cynicism is a curable disease; bitterness can become sweet refreshing water again. To heal from cynicism, you must remove the tumors of improper attachments, begin a therapeutic protocol of rest, and choose your own health over constant busyness and unrealistic expectations.

How? You must plan a new, more sustainable pace. You must make rest part of your method. Capture every negative thought circling the drain of your mind — capture, and then release it. There is always an element of truth in negative thoughts, so why would you release the truth? The answer is this: trying to separate the small element of truth from the larger negative thought destroys your belief in the truth. So, release it all. The truth will survive without your help. It will never abandon you.

There is hope, with new methods. The transformation from bitter to sweet requires you to sacrifice your own pride, to rise again from the ashes of your previous failed attempts, and reinvest yourself again, more humbly, into the dreams that Life has entrusted to you.

Never, ever, ever doubt your Calling simply because of a lack of results. Your Calling carries the blueprint of your strongest soul, the plan for your Great Work in the world. Do not doubt that you are Called, just because the results have not fully emerged. Your life is meant to be an adventure of creative exploration into a wide variety of methods and means to fulfill your Calling.

You now know the swamps of cynicism well enough. It is time to move on. Because if a cynic is a wounded idealist, then a mentor is a recovered cynic. Begin again, with rest as your means, as a way of life.

What will your own therapeutic protocol of rest look like? What allows you to detach, let go, sleep better and more, recover, recharge... what inspires you? Choose at least five of the following options, and follow them for the next ninety days – or replace them with your own:

- At least ten minutes every day, alone in quiet meditation
- At least ten minutes each day, freehand writing or journaling
- At least thirty minutes of active exercise, five days each week
- No artificial light or screen time three hours before bed, enjoy candles instead
- At least nine consecutive hours in bed each night, with the goal of eight asleep
- Better nutrition and fewer stimulants, reduce caffeine, sugars, and processed foods

Part 6

WORK ETHIC AND REST

A strong, sustainable work ethic needs an equally strong rest ethic.

Rest is not the opposite of work.

Fear is the opposite of work.

Fear adds unnecessary tension, pressure, and conflict to an otherwise healthy, productive, and valuable work ethic.

Perhaps what we really need is not less work, but a stronger, more sustainable rest ethic.

Fearless

Self-criticism is nothing more than fear of your own inner strength.
Self-doubt is fear of others' evaluations of you.
"Too busy" is just your deep, hidden fear of change.
At least half of your life is about learning... "Do not be afraid."
Fear, not work, is the opposite of rest.

— STRATEGIC REST —

Make a list of the three most difficult work situations of your entire career.

What fears did you experience during those situations that drove you to work longer hours, lose sleep, or lose motivation to do your best work?

Take the time to explore each of these fears and understand how they may still lie dormant, ready to flare up again in another future crisis.

Now, test your heart to see how a deeper level of rest and trust could allow you to meet your next crisis with less stress and more inner strength. Journal your thoughts to gain wisdom when you look back at this moment of reflection.

Motivation

What motivates your most urgent work: hope or fear?

When fear leads, people are pushed aside, run over, diminished. The proverbial "fire drill" prevails, as long hours and heroic efforts are required to complete what could have been a peaceful and successful project. When fear motivates, there is never enough time, quality suffers, and relationships barely survive.

When hope leads, the entire team focuses on the good that will be accomplished when each member plays their proper part, serving each other with generosity and respect, learning and adapting together as necessary to fulfill the vision. When hope motivates, good people do excellent work, with minimal stress, tension, and conflict.

To rest is to make a statement for hope. Of course, there is always a chance that things may not work out; something bad may happen; you may not have the strength to pull through and finish, to accomplish the whole plan. Those are constants, with either fear or hope. Fear magnifies those concerns into imminent risks. Hope does not ignore those concerns; it just puts them in their proper place.

Without awareness of fear, there is no wisdom, no contingency planning.

Without awareness of fear, you get sloppy and careless.

But without awareness of hope, there can be no rest.

The question for you today is: will you obsess over some distant worst-case scenario and allow fear to motivate, or focus on the present potential goodness in your life, imperfect as it may be, and allow hope to motivate?

Hope is not the absence of fear, but the expectation of goodness.

— STRATEGIC REST —

What is motivating the most urgent tasks in front of you right now... some distant worst-case scenario (fear), or the present potential goodness in your life (hope)?

Addiction

The worship of work sustains a spirit of poverty, but the practice of rest is a trusting statement of freedom and abundance.

If you work from within a spirit of poverty, your work itself can easily become a narcotic to numb your guilt or hide your fear over financial deficits. You work and worry and wither away to dig out of debt, to make the next payment, to buy the next Thing. But the root problem remains: as soon as one goal is met, another big "want" takes its place.

But what of your soul? Has work become your god, your provider, the only means to address your wants and needs? Are there alternatives? A simpler lifestyle? A more peaceful demeanor, not just at work, but at home as well?

The workaholic must learn to trust again. To wean themselves from believing that fast-paced urgency and desperation will solve their problems, help them get what they want, or cover their brokenness.

Allow yourself to feel the full weight of responsibility, the total reality of your present position. The finances. The deadlines. The demands.

Accept it, just as it is right now, in the present moment.

Release any judgment of whether this present reality is good or bad – either, at all.

Then redirect your thoughts about your present wants or needs, goals or concerns, to a new and different place. Rather than pouring yourself into a hectic work focus, guide your thoughts to gratitude and contentment for what you have today, and trust and faith that tomorrow will dawn with still more to be grateful for. Let your work be an expression of service and care for others, not just a means to get what you want.

Gratitude and contentment won't pay the bills, but an addiction to work will not sustain your soul.

And work itself is not the problem, anyway; you need to replace the reason you work – old fears, pain, or desperation – with trust and peace.

Work and rest are equals and allies, not enemies at odds.

Take them in turn. Day in, day out. Rest and work.

– STRATEGIC REST –

"If we want to live a Wholehearted life, we have to become intentional about cultivating rest and plan, and we must work to let go of exhaustion as a status symbol and productivity as self-worth."
— Brené Brown, Ph.D.

Slacking off

Letting go of tension and stress is not the same as slacking off from work.

Every effective effort begins and ends with healthy rest, like bookends on either side of the work. You start rested, do good work, and then rest again.

Your work itself looks different when you have rested well. It is less frenetic, stressed, and anxious.

Your rest looks different when you have worked well. It is less guilt-ridden and healthier – you do not need to reach for substitutes to true relaxation.

The key is to know when to transition from work, to rest, and back to work… and how to excel at all three: the work, the rest, and the transitions.

Deep rest may look different for each of us. But the need to rest deeply is not only common to each of us, it is vital to our mental, emotional, and physical health. Just as each of us prefers different foods, each of us may prefer different forms or methods of rest. But food and rest, work and play, are the basis of health, for everyone. If we ignore food, or choose the wrong forms of food, our immune system suffers. But if we ignore rest, or choose the wrong form, our value system suffers.

– STRATEGIC REST –

Are you the exception to all of this talk about rest?

There is a particular form of defensiveness in which we insist that we are different than others. That we do not need rest, as others need rest. Maybe not as much. Maybe not as badly.

Here is the lie: rest makes us vulnerable to a poor performance evaluation. We are afraid that someone might point out that all we have done, to the best of our ability, is still not enough to make us acceptable.

Strategic Rest offers you grace and transformation here. As you allow deep rest, you act as if you are valuable and worthy of respect, even while resting… while not performing or delivering some valuable service for someone – even for yourself.

What is unique about you is not your lack of need for deep rest, but your unique Calling in life – that community you are Called to serve, and your unique way of working in that place. Your rest may not look like mine, but it has the same effect: it reminds you that you are vulnerable, that you are worthy of love, apart from your performance, and that there is so much more to life than clicking "done."

Hope

We see our deepest hopes as if they were fish beneath the surface of a calm pool, swimming around in a different world than ours, independently of us, skittish and inscrutable.

We do not understand how they live. What they want. Even whether those hopes which form our dreams and visions would be worth the effort, the change, and risk to make them real.

So truly, we are uncertain whether we want to become those hopes at all. It feels good to entertain them, but… that water looks cold. We are not sure how we might breathe, down there. As an outsider to our own deepest desires, we can see their boundaries, their limits. To achieve what we envision requires leaving the world we know today. And we hesitate.

You will stay where you are until you truly know what you truly want.

But once you know, nothing will stop you.

– STRATEGIC REST –

Have you rested long enough to develop intimacy with your deepest hopes? Not just your goals, but your hopes, about a different life connected to meaning and purpose?

Have you rested here long enough to decide whether they truly are part of you?

To decide which of them are your path, for life?

To decide… and start in that direction?

To decide… nothing can stop you from moving towards that one, especially?

Uphill

The road to hell is paved with good intentions. It is downhill all the way. Status quo. De facto. Coasting along. Old thinking that has become automated… leading to atrophy.

The path to 'done' – for your Work, your Art, your Calling – is also paved with good intentions. It is uphill all the way... sweaty, risky, and powered by hard work, even as self-doubt and fear of rejection nip at your heels.

Rest is an effective discipline for world changers. It is designed to refresh and renew and reset your perspective, to cleanse and re-energize you for the road ahead. Uphill.

Do not forget to rest, as you climb.

— STRATEGIC REST —

There are places to rest every day, even on a long uphill push.
Take a look around.
Where is your next one?
And how do you plan to rest, when you get there?

Step by step

Persistence is the only way you will ever accomplish the worthiest work you are meant to do. Dogged, raw, sweaty persistence is the glue that assembles the pieces of any great work.

But without rest, persistence is impossible – fatigue drains your stamina.

Rest allows persistence to emerge.

One step at a time, we work… rest… work… rest… and so, persist.

– STRATEGIC REST –

Rest and work are not enemies.

They are not even opposites.

They are friends.

The opposite of diligent work is not rest – it is lazy weakness.

The opposite of Strategic Rest is not work, but pointless effort motivated by fear.

Start with rest

"…and the evening and the morning were the first day."

Our ancestors did not rest at the end of their days, at the end of their weeks, at the end of their seasons. Rest was not an afterthought for them. They rested before they began. They started with rest. They laid down their swords and scythes to gain the wisdom of perspective that can only come from a time of peace and objective detachment from pulling weeds and fighting battles.

In early civilizations and ancient wisdom literature, each day began at sunset, not in the morning. Each week started with a full day of rest. Eating and drinking and sleeping during ten-day feasts helped to initiate and celebrate new seasons on the calendar.

It is wise to rest first, then work… instead of beginning with work, and leaving rest for later, as time allows.

Rest is the predicate, not the reward.

Rest is the preparation, not the result.

Rest is the first priority, not the last.

– STRATEGIC REST –

Starting with rest is not just a matter of an even swap of blocks of time – rest, then work… instead of work, then rest. No, the practice of starting with rest greatly increases your output and improves your outlook during each work session.

When you view each work session as beginning with rest… each day begins with sleep, work sessions begin with a break, the subconscious mind is left free to solve problems and frame tasks and context for your work ahead, without the demands of immediate production. So then, when you do begin work, the quality is often higher, and your output is greater.

Part 7

COMMUNITY

Few of us were ever destined to live alone.

Connecting with others and sharing experiences is part of being human.

As we seek deeper rest, we realize the importance of community as a source of safety, teamwork, and support. In terms of personal transformation, a trusted community can help us rewrite old outdated scripts that result in strain and tension, into more open and present realities that foster new ideas, creativity, and productivity.

We may claim to be "too busy" to invest time each week in our vital friendships. We may propose that we are introverts and prefer to keep our distance. But at the core, every excuse to building relationships boils down to a single dynamic most of us wish we could easily dismiss: our own dogma.

Dogma is like an old, run down urban slum made up of our oldest, least examined beliefs. That slum can be divided into distinct boroughs surrounded by concrete walls, and mostly run by ideological thugs. Some of those boroughs border the old, dogmatic territory of others nearby; but those are not friends over there... they are competitors at best, and threats in the darkest night.

A few miles further away in any direction, you will find the tidier communities and manicured lawns of healthier creeds, neighborly denominations who are a little less messy. These are our public agreements – areas where we have all decided to just play nice.

But across the fields and down by the river is where you will find the best dancing, music, food, and wine. Here, spiritual gypsies carve out a rich existence, refusing to be pinned down, but always willing to make new friends, and protecting their old ones like a strong, primal tribe.

And there you will find me, by the fire, near the children, singing and smiling with a full heart. Here is a seat for you, too, if you'd like it...

Help

"A single twig breaks, but the bundle of twigs is strong."
– Chief Tecumseh

If it is too much for you... then you were never meant to carry it alone.
You were always meant to live and work in groups defined by trust.
Two are better than one, and three are better than two.
To find sustainable rest, you must find a community committed to your cause for the long haul.
At least one who is more experienced than you.
At least one who is less experienced.
And at least one who is near where you are today.
This is the community in which your Calling can emerge in greater detail.

– STRATEGIC REST –

"Too busy" is a lonely place to hide. It is worthwhile to stop, and rest, enjoy life, and connect with friends. Not just once in a while, but as a way of life.

The faceless cause

When you fight for a faceless cause, for the purity of principles or the theory of flawless fundamentals, you miss the clues to know when you should stop fighting. You often feel borderline combative, hypersensitive to the definitions of things, insensitive to the hearts of others. When you fight only for theories and ideals, you will not be able to rest until everyone you meet agrees with you.

But the truth is, if you are fighting for a faceless, nameless cause, then you are probably not even on the front lines of that battle – in spite of the passion of your beliefs. Because on the front lines and under fire… nobody fights only for a cause, but also for the friend right next to them.

Every effective fight has real faces and names behind it. And if you must fight for what is right, you will be most effective when your tactics are specific and personal, not just some high-minded ideal that even you cannot yourself truly sustain.

The faceless cause leads to untenable situations, defensiveness, criticism, and chronic interpersonal conflict.

Instead, fight for your friends, and for theirs… for them and theirs and what you all believe is right. When you have won freedom for these, you will know for sure, and you will rest.

– STRATEGIC REST –

Are you more inclined to join a cause, or to assist a person struggling within that cause?

No agenda

Your most treasured friendships hint at the essence of rest: they are characterized by a natural, fluid, fully accepting awareness of what is here and now, without judgment. You are free to enjoy these friends' love, without any agenda, demand, or expectation of them.

The same is true in solitude: Rest is characterized by easy, fluid, fully accepting awareness of what is here and now, without judgment. It is self-love, without any agenda, demand, or expectation of yourself.

— STRATEGIC REST —

"There's something magical about doing nothing, and we don't do it often enough."

– Tsh Oxenreider, Notes from a Blue Bike

In the dark

Your guard was down, and you were hit hard.
Too quickly, you forgot who you really are.
You listened to The Lies again and lashed out in anger.
Afterward, shadows lengthened, and your deepest fears re-emerged.
You were not meant to be here alone.
You cannot tend all these deep wounds by yourself.
When you take refuge, do not go alone to find safety.
Your trusted friends hold a true mirror.
You and your friends – you were made for each other.
They will help you find deep rest.

– STRATEGIC REST –

Feel free to refuse to walk through these four dark places alone this week:
- **Contradiction, in which you feel compelled to argue with fools.**
- **Comparison, in which you always fall short in some form.**
- **Criticism, in which you focus on what is wrong, instead of what is good.**
- **Imagined conversations, in which you waste useful energy in useless arguments.**

Dogma

"We judge ourselves by our intentions and others by their behaviour."
– Stephen M.R. Covey, *The Speed of Trust*

At best, you are only ever about half right, about half the time. But only a few close friends will ever tell you to your face.

So, just chill out. Double-check your facts. Consider other perspectives. Honor the experience of others. Be humble. Listen to them. Respect them.

Because dogma only offers a downhill slide to broken relationships.

– STRATEGIC REST –

Enjoy an hour this week connecting with someone you respect.
Listen twice as much as you speak.
No agenda, no judgment, no comparisons – just fully participate in their story.

Abundance

Destiny does not reward the weary soul.

Instead, it offers periods of rest as waypoints on your path to a unique service and sacrifice that will, indeed, change your world.

If you cannot rest, you cannot see.

If you cannot see, you cannot distinguish friend from foe.

And if you do not know your friends, you will never defeat your enemies, or claim the place that is meant for you.

Rest is your way of life, your doorway to a spirit of growth and abundance.

— STRATEGIC REST —

What does abundance mean, to you?

And how do constant weariness and fatigue prevent you from stepping into your own idea of abundance?

What might happen if you reached for your calendar right now, and planned an extended time to recover from weariness and fatigue, strain, tension and overwork?

Plan some waypoints of rest, soon, so you will be better able to see what is good, connect with your friends, and claim what is meant for you – what is good.

Take deliberate steps to rest.

Toughness

The warrior is not always powerful, brave, and strong.

Especially when wounded.

Warriors know that rest is a tactical advantage, and thus a strategic weapon.

There is a time to fight hard, and there is a time to step back, remove the armor, and let your allies see and help tend to the wounds.

— STRATEGIC REST —

What type of 'tough' is right for you now?

The tough warrior who is fighting well, with endurance, persistence, and strength?

Or the tough warrior who is strong enough to be vulnerable… lay down the sword, lower the defenses, and accept help, comfort, and rest from allies?

Heaviness

"The truth, without grace, is not really the truth."
– Ron Graves

I saw an old-fashioned measuring scale, standing alone on a table in the center of a dark room. On its base was carved a single word: "Justice." Atop a thin center post, there balanced a brass cross arm, with bowls hung from chains on either side.

The bowl on the left bore my name. The bowl on the right bore his.

Then as I watched, a handful of coins were dropped into my bowl, and the scale tipped violently. Instantly, I felt the imbalance in my heart itself – and in my body and bones. My vision blurred, my thoughts confused, as I watched the thin center post strain under the new weight on the scale. My bowl hung low on the left.

A Voice said, "This is your fault. You are the guilty one. You must pay a price for your wrongs." I shrunk back, afraid. I felt sick, dizzy, and incapable of sorting out what to do next. The cost of my guilt and its effects nearly paralyzed me, as I considered how wrong the weight of my faults, the unfairness of his empty bowl.

Then the Voice called, "You must decide how you will balance the scale."

Another pile of coins dropped to the table. More coins. More provision. In my current frame of mind, I knew I must balance the scale, or I would be unable to function nearly at all.

I reached for the pile of coins, steadying myself, and dropped a few into his bowl on the right. The cross arm swung back; some balance restored. My vision cleared. I felt the exhilaration of relief. A cool anger swept through me, and I picked up a few more coins, dropped them into his bowl. But now the thin post bent nearly in half, straining under the weight of the coins on both sides. I saw that to fully restore balance and regain health would require that I add all the remaining coins to his bowl.

But then there would be no coins left. Not for him. Not for me.

And the Voice said, "There is a better way to restore balance."

We each carry a sense of Justice, like an old-fashioned scale in our minds, our bowl on the left, their bowl on the right, hanging in delicate balance.

Our mistakes pile high. The guilt we accumulate in life weighs us down, bringing confusion and sapping our strength. To balance the scales, we place blame on others – it is not all our fault! We pile on the wrong, hoping for relief.

But Justice is bent. Our soul is impoverished. Relationships bear the cost.

And then we wonder, "Why do I feel so heavy today, like I am carrying weight everywhere I go? Why the confusion? Why this deep anger?"

I looked again at the scale in the room. I decided to forgive, myself and him. I carefully removed a coin from my bowl and a coin from his. Then another, and another. One piece at a time, as I forgave myself, and him, the scale was unburdened.

I had dealt with my guilt. And I had stopped blaming him.

Freedom is living with an empty scale. No residual guilt. No residual blame.

The first to apologize is the bravest.

The first to forgive is the strongest.

The first to forget is the happiest.

— STRATEGIC REST —

Where do you sense heaviness, still — the shame of guilt, or the indignity of blame?

Has the time come now to release that heaviness, so you can move on?

Thermostats and thermometers

"The plain fact is that the planet does not need more successful people. But it does desperately need more peacemakers, healers, restorers, storytellers, and lovers of every kind. It needs people who live well in their places. It needs people of moral courage willing to join the fight to make the world habitable and humane. And these qualities have little to do with success as we have defined it."   – Dalai Lama

People behave one of two ways: as thermometers or thermostats.

Thermometers are managers and observers.

Thermostats are leaders and contributors.

A thermometer shifts and changes based on the environment nearby. When there is negativity and anger in the air, a thermometer reflects them in full strength. When fear and criticism go unchecked, chronic dysfunction can polarize and paralyze entire teams of otherwise competent and capable people. Those people choose sides. Peace suffers. Healing stops. Excellence is no longer the focus, or even an option. Where irresponsibility reigns, there can be no heroic story of prevailing love.

But a thermostat places limits on extremes. The thermostat itself does no work – it carries no stress or strain, no tension or effort. Just as a thermometer observes, so also a thermostat observes what is going on... but then a thermostat responds. It activates a new and greater energy to overcome the imbalance in the air. It refuses to blindly accept things as they are: once a limit is reached, the thermostat initiates a change. Period. This is the respected, determined peacemaker. The relentless healer. The careful, sensitive, competent leader. These are our heroes at work.

– STRATEGIC REST –

Do you enter your world of work each day as a thermostat or a thermometer? Do you merely reflect the atmosphere nearby, or do you respond with meaningful limits and actions that build trust and safety in the team?

Ignore everyone

Everyone does not matter.
Everyone's feedback, input, and criticism do not matter.
You cannot please everyone.
You cannot serve everyone.
You cannot help everyone.
You cannot make everyone understand, happy, productive, or well.
So, ignore 'everyone.'
Become an expert at serving the few you are called to serve – those who instinctively come near and allow you to share in their journey.
And let all the others serve all the others.

– STRATEGIC REST –

It is impossible to find deep rest while nursing an approval addiction.

Consistency

Be kind and gracious today.
Even when it is hard.
You paid far too much for a legitimate claim on humility, to ruin it in a moment of ignorant pride.

– STRATEGIC REST –

**To be kind to your enemy is the greatest courage.
To be kind first is leadership.**

Maturity

When you first began, you were out to change the world.

A few mishaps later, it occurred to you that you may need to change some things in yourself.

Then, maturity is about learning to accept yourself, as you really are.

And next... love teaches you to accept the world, as it really is.

— STRATEGIC REST —

How well do you understand your role in the fulfillment of your Calling?

How mature is that understanding?

When a Calling matures, it is purified of demands that others must change in order to participate.

An invitation to participate without prejudice is evidence of love.

Creators win

Critics and consumers are always at the mercy of creators.
Choose your role wisely.

– STRATEGIC REST –

"Create a life for yourself that you absolutely love. And fall in love with the person you are becoming. Extend grace to yourself. Laugh at yourself and trust your instincts. Embrace the concept of mistakes. Realize they are unavoidable... Actually, you shouldn't want to avoid mistakes. They tell you more and more about the person that you truly are! Take risks and dive in even when you aren't sure it's safe. What is that saying? 'Nothing ventured, nothing gained'? If you don't step out of your comfort zone you will never find yourself in greener pastures."
– Jessica Goforth Francis

Part 8

DECIDE

Everything changes, but rarely on your schedule, or according to your plan. That is why flexibility, acceptance, and resilience are keys to your emotional health. The strong demonstrate their strength, not only in their ability to persist, but also in their ability to adapt or start over, again and again.

Strategic Rest is the trusted ally of the strong.

Is it time now to decide that you will change the way you work and rest?

Is it time to commit to Strategic Rest, as part of your everyday life?

And is that a decision you can make now, or a thousand decisions you will make as you persist in the direction of your Calling?

You already know

The more agonizing the question you have been mulling over... the more likely you already know the answer but are avoiding it because change is difficult.

You probably know, you just haven't acted on it yet.

Rest is not delay or hesitation. It is not laziness or irresponsibility.

There is a time to rest, but also a time to press forward again with sweat and strength and courage.

— STRATEGIC REST —

"On the plains of hesitation bleach the bones of countless millions who, at the dawn of victory, sat down to wait... and waiting, died."
– George Cecil

The next step

You do know. You just haven't stepped up yet.

The real question is not, "What should I do," but "Why haven't I done it yet?"

It is not because you have not had the time.

Most likely, it is fear.

The most common chronic fear is that you are inadequate to your own Calling. You readily disqualify yourself from the very thing you are Called to do, as a means of wiggling free of the obligation to act beyond the self-doubts that have held you back for most of your life.

It is the perfect excuse: "There must be someone else to do this Great Work – because I am so wholly inadequate for it."

But that is wrong. You are it. There is no one else for this.

You do already know the next step.

The courage to take that step will never come before you need it, but rather as you step out. As you move forward, damn those fears, courage appears.

Courage is the visible smoke of your old self-doubts burning in the wake of deliberate action, as you plow ahead, tears streaming down your face, towards the light of your Calling.

– STRATEGIC REST –

You do know that the fears that prevent you from stepping into your calling are only paper thin, right? On the other side of your defiant act of love to step up, step in, and get involved... is an exhilarating newness – a risky, tenuous, fresh place, where perspectives shift, selfish old habits become useless, and you find new friendships and deeper partnerships.

So, what does all of that cost you? Not much; just all of that false sense of security you have used to wall off those you are called to serve.

Endless search

Do not allow your search for meaning within a difficult situation to become an excuse to avoid making a tough decision. The search ends when opportunity meets risk and demands a decision. At the point of decision, meaning can wait; you will find the meaning you seek as hindsight, later.

Today, decide.

Move forward.

— STRATEGIC REST —

"There will come a time when you believe everything is finished. That will be the beginning."

— Louis L'Amour

Testing

It will take longer.
It will cost more.
It will be harder.
It will hurt worse.
It will be more complicated.
It will look different than you envisioned.
It will require more than you planned.
It will not turn out exactly as you thought.
So, what... are you going to quit?
If it is worth doing, then it is worth pushing thru.
This struggle is not for anyone else.
It is for you, to prove to yourself that this is the path you must follow.
If you can quit – go for it. Bail out. Feel free to ditch anything you can. Or keep it. Because those things that you see as optional, probably are. It is the things you cannot quit that deserve your attention. Because they point to your Calling.

– STRATEGIC REST –

If you cannot, in good conscience, refuse to work on something, then it is either helping you avoid your Calling, or pointing you toward it. Make those things you cannot easily quit the focus of your own self-education over the next few weeks. And here are two key questions:

1. Why is this work so important to me?
2. Who benefits from it?

Uncertainty

Uncertainty is best welcomed as an instructor or coach.

Uncertainty raises strong questions and presents a series of small challenges that serve as stepping-stones towards the wisdom and discoveries that legitimize your success when it arrives.

Certainty is not only the enemy of faith, but the sham diploma of a student who is cheating their way thru the School of Life.

— STRATEGIC REST —

Embrace the questions.
Accept the challenges.
Learn the lessons.
Reject false certainty.
Do the work to earn your success, one doubt-filled, courageous decision at a time.

Avoidance

What if the very thing you have resisted for years... that thing you have tried so hard to avoid, reshape, and re-characterize... what if that idea, direction, or aspect is your next willing step on the path towards your Calling?

What if stepping into that thing you have resisted will open up some huge untapped potential in the niche you are meant to serve next?

If so, the question goes beyond: "Why am I avoiding that thing...?"

Deeper, it is: "Why can't I let go of it?"

Because it is you... you are the one that is holding back, avoiding it somehow. And you might be avoiding it because you know something, instinctively. Perhaps you know there is huge potential there, bigger than you have ever seen.

– STRATEGIC REST –

What is the aspect or label or title or position or invitation or expectation... what is it that has consistently been put before you by others? That thing you have consistently resisted?

Is it possible that expectation or invitation or position or title or label or aspect... might represent for you a personal challenge that could lead you to a professional breakthrough?

You get to choose your lens

What if the thing that you believe is the problem, is not really the problem?

What if the only real problem, is the way you see that thing?

What if you let go of it... let go of your assessment, but also your assumption that there may be something you should do about it?

– STRATEGIC REST –

What if you just let all of that go, right now?

Because letting it all go might solve the real problem: your outdated assumptions.

Overthinking things

Indecision is unrest.
Overthinking is overrated.
Life is less about making the right decisions, and more about making your decisions right.
That is the difference between dogma and grace.
Immerse yourself in quiet rest and listen.
Then trust your gut, decide, and go.
Let grace make your best decisions, the right decisions.

— STRATEGIC REST —

What significant decisions are you facing today?

Now, consider those decisions in the light of your Calling... which options will bring you closer to those you serve?

Every decision you face will change shape and form when evaluated within the context of your Calling, instead of the immediate convenience, comfort, circumstances, or present limitations of your everyday life.

Part 9

CALLING

Some call it destiny, others call it purpose in life, cause, or fate.

But few live their lives without feeling it, without some sense that they are connected to something bigger than themselves, that there is some force at work moving them towards a determined path or direction.

I believe it is impossible to fully embrace the concept of your Calling while living a work-saturated, weary, tense, day-to-day existence. But when we make changes to allow for Strategic Rest, we find a renewed sense of purpose, an intention to serve wants to emerge. It begs for conscious space – for deliberate acts and full acceptance.

Make space for it, even if you are not able to fully describe exactly what your Calling is… it becomes undeniably present to you.

The connection between Calling and Strategic Rest is tangible. I have come to recognize that my Calling is not a fixed or finite thing… it evolves and adapts based on the world around me, and my own growth and personal development. If that is true, then the necessary changes I make to adopt rest as a way of life will directly impact both my awareness of, and my ability to actively participate in, my own unique Calling in life.

Signs

Three signs you are near your Calling:
1. The task before you is so big you could not do it alone.
2. You care so much you would be willing to die for it.
3. You realize you no longer need a script at all.

— STRATEGIC REST —

Sit quietly for a while and ponder these three. Just quiet your mind and allow your heart to speak to each, in turn. Do not try to direct or control it – just let it speak, until it is finished.

Perspective

Here is a sure sign you have caught a glimpse of your Calling: self-pity seems so, so trite.

The only proper perspective for an evaluation of your strengths and weaknesses is the context of your Calling.

Only here do your weaknesses recede to their proper irrelevance, lending you humility and encouraging healthy boundaries.

Only here do your strengths lend you credibility and the capacity to work in your area of service.

Only within the context of your Calling do your present limitations shift from a list of complaints, to a set of steppingstones that lead you to deeper trust and meaning.

Only within the context of your Calling do your accomplishments humble you to press even more deeply into the service of those around you.

– STRATEGIC REST –

Consider your strengths and weaknesses, not by way of comparison with others, but in terms of sacrifice towards those you are Called to serve. How does that context of your Calling change your notion of your most prominent personality traits?

Deep pain

"Remember your dreams and fight for them. You must know what you want from life. There is just one thing that makes your dream become impossible: the fear of failure." – Paulo Coelho

Your deepest pain is the compass that points towards your Calling.

Your deepest joy will be to turn your deepest pain on its head, through working in your Calling.

Hiding your deepest pain in shame will prevent you from ever reaching your Calling.

The whole point of pain in life is to drive you towards redemption, towards the fulfillment of your Calling that turns your deepest pain into your deepest joy.

– STRATEGIC REST –

Deep pain demands a response.

What does rest look like for you, in the presence of pain?

What does your Calling look like for you, in the presence of pain?

How do the practice of rest and joy in the presence of pain effect your relationships with others?

The shadow

When you turned away from Life, that is when you found yourself surrounded by fear, cold, and darkness.
And when you turn back, warmth and light surround you again.
You did not invent these realities; you have discovered Truth.
Fear is the shadow cast by your Calling.

– STRATEGIC REST –

What do your fears say to you?
Now, what does your Calling say?

Digging out

You will find your Calling along the border of The Mess of your Past and the Present Moment. Though it is buried under layers of Pain and Self-Doubt, it is not too deep... Selfless Service will uncover it with Honesty, in short order. And when you dig deep there, you will find a rich vein of Meaning that you can explore to the end of your days.

Begin a personal life timeline. Choose a timeframe – a year, five years, ten years or fifty, and draw them across the top of a page. Now, working backwards from your present reality into the past, begin to put lines on paper to represent places you have worked, lived, travelled, and studied. Include milestones for significant life events. Take an hour or two, and simply lay out your past in clear strokes, showing changes over time.

Notice where your thoughts and feelings begin to pool, around specific events full of joy or pain. But keep moving. Keep drawing. Keep adding events and transitions, both mundane and important.

Over the next few weeks, begin to journal and unpack some perspective from the overall timeline you have drawn. Fears that never took form... hopes that have yet to come true... surprises and events that seemed insurmountable, yet you walked through them. Recall the people who have helped you along the way, opened doors, offered support.

And now, can you see the life of your Calling over these past months and years? Can you see yourself moving towards it, avoiding it, playing with it and experimenting? Can you begin to notice how Life itself has placed you or moved you along, despite your reluctance to change, or your fear of stepping out and taking risks?

Now, come back to the present moment... what perspective and help does your history offer as hope for the coming weeks and months, as you continue to move forward, in selfless sacrifice, towards your Calling?

Insignificance

Man first sought safety, fire, water, food, and shelter.

Then, the comforts of home.

Then, meaningful work.

But lately, we have sacrificed too much for Significance and Legacy.

What if your unique Calling in life requires you to remain Insignificant?

To leave no recognizable Legacy?

Would you resist, and insist on sacrificing your life and Calling on the altar of your own Significance?

Or would you be willing, instead, to serve quietly, invisibly, as one of many who are simply satisfied with the sweat on their brow as they pursue their Calling from day to day… and let history write your story's ending?

— STRATEGIC REST —

How would your work and rest change, if you deliberately turned your back on any concern for your own significance, for your concept of impact or legacy?

Where you belong

To wrestle with the weight of your own failures, in the darkness of self-doubt and broken dreams, in the narrow alley where love and good intentions are mistaken for selfish ambition… to fight here, blindly, with an uncertain outcome, for what is right… seems pure foolishness. Here, you fight not just for some romantic ideal, but for your very existence. For the right to stand your ground, occupy a place, and stake a claim – because, for all your faults… this is where you belong.

You will never meet a strong person with an easy past.

You must ask no less of yourself.

– STRATEGIC REST –

How have you disrespected your own struggle? Can you take a deep breath, step back, and begin to appreciate your own work, over the years, to do your best, push thru pain, uncertainty, and discomfort… to own your mistakes, and keep stepping up to serve the world in the place of your Calling?

Big leagues

Eventually, the proper rhythm of rest and work within your Calling may land you in the presence of kings for a time. And all the skills and lessons that got you there will become non-optional if you wish to remain in their court.

The same rest that sustains you through private victories, prepares you for public excellence.

— STRATEGIC REST —

One of the most illogical motivational truths in the world is this:
"You cannot get what you want by pushing, pulling or grasping... but if you work selflessly in your Calling, all things become possible."

Struggle

Your vision holds a promise of deep grace for you, personally.

Because any worthwhile vision, requires struggle.

It is the struggle, not the vision, that carves out the depths of your soul.

That depth, formed by suffering and strength, is the credibility to move in your Calling – it is the only credential you need.

But the struggle itself is not your work. If you focus on the struggle – seek it, serve it, slave for it – you will only wear yourself out, without gaining any new ground.

Strategic Rest accepts every step along the path of Life, with grace.

It accepts the work, the struggle, the suffering, the mystery, and the joy... before you see the vision of your Calling fulfilled.

– STRATEGIC REST –

Do not serve the struggle; accept it.

Instead, serve the vision by practicing the promise of its grace, in the struggle of today.

Finish this sentence…

"I could be working today to bring clean water and basic education to impoverished communities around the world, saving thousands of lives, but right now, it is more important for me to…"

– STRATEGIC REST –

Journal your response…

Keep moving

Unsure of the outcome, yet still you push on.

Why?

Not because you are certain of what lies ahead, but because you still have something left unsaid.

Exhaustion cannot deflate your message.

Cynicism cannot smother it.

Prejudice cannot block it.

You continue to show up, step up, and play the game… simply because your heart cannot stay silent.

The duty of your Calling is irrevocable.

That is the core of your persistence.

— STRATEGIC REST —

"Hope begins in the dark, the stubborn hope that if I just show up and try to do the right thing, the dawn will come."
– Anne Lamott

Calling is not a talisman to suffering

Listen well. Focus on the fundamentals. Commit to good hard work and leverage the wisdom of those with more experience. Take everything in stride. Find a mentor – someone who can help steady your hand. Be humble and quiet and mind your own business. Never ever criticize anyone for anything. Brag on people who do good stuff and overlook others' mistakes. Above all – be honest and trustworthy, the genuine article.

All this will not work all the time. The world can be cold, unforgiving, and violent. Do not be surprised when you are unfairly criticized or misunderstood and falsely accused when you did what you thought was the right thing. Do your best to tell the truth about what happened but own your mistakes. Then, dust yourself off and move on. Do what you know you are called to do. Be the person you want to look up to thirty years from now.

Your Calling is not a talisman to suffering; persist.

– STRATEGIC REST –

Your calling is not just to do something. It is to be something.

If you want to make a difference – if you want to find your groove, get your mojo back, make some Great Change in the world – you must let go of the stuff that pulls you away from your true course.

Consider what moves you towards your Calling, and what keeps you away.

Collect the first, ditch the other.

Now, rise

Rise, weak one, to take your place among the strong.

Rise, overlooked one… neglected and ignored, as a newly courageous peacemaker who forbids others to manipulate you to selfish ends.

Rise, beaten one, to become a protector yourself… you who have known the blunt end of strength, and therefore, you whom we trust to carry great power with gentleness and humility.

Rise, you, now… to watch day and night over the innocent, as a living watch guard, confronting threats with: 'Do rightly, or else…'

Rise, now. Do not fear. Allow the pain of your past wounds to fuel the preparation of your inner Calling.

Rise, now, alone, and yet still in the dark. Do not wait until the lights come on for you. The world has not prepared you a stage. You must begin now, with nothing, building, working, preparing in the dark.

Now, rise.

We need you.

– STRATEGIC REST –

Take a glance back over your journal, in which you have explored these ideas of Strategic Rest. Message a friend and plan a time to sit and share, no agenda, just observe and be open and connect over the idea of work and rest and the importance of caring for yourself as well as your Calling.

And, rest.

Strategically.

For you.

For your community.

For your Calling.

Rest.

EPILOGUE

Just Let Go of the Damn Banana

For over year now, I have been practicing Strategic Rest, and I am still very much learning these lessons. I would not be exaggerating to say it has been one of the best things that ever happened to my work life.

Rest is a practice... a set of learned skills to rely on; with frequent use, they become more instinctive and natural to us.

I have noticed other benefits to the practice of Strategic Rest. I have learned that the real secret to sustainable productivity is more than goals and education and optimism – it is you, being well. It is, quite literally, your own health and well-being, as a valuable person. It is learning that the best thing you can ever do for those around you, whom you serve, is:

...to eat, well.

...to exercise, well.

...to work, well.

...to rest, well.

...to think, well.

...to feel, well.

...to adapt, well.

...to change, well.

...to lead, well.

...to love, well.

As I have spoken with colleagues and friends around the world about Strategic Rest, I have realized there is one common, sinister snare that most often prevents us from practicing Strategic Rest. What is it?

The easiest way to capture a monkey is to hide a banana in a jug that is chained to a tree. The monkey is attracted by the jug and the chain... curious, really, and fascinated at how these attachments work. But then... oh, there is a banana inside! Right there, I can just reach in and grab it! An immediate reward. How tasty it would be! It does not matter that the trees overhead have dozens more bananas – it is the banana I can only get from this one contraption that has captured my attention. And so, the monkey reaches into the jug and grasps the banana... and his clenched fist is too large to exit the mouth of the jug. Infuriating! If he could only get that banana out! He can feel it... smell it... touch it. But he cannot possess it. He cannot benefit from the fruit of the trap. Ever. The trap is there to hold him long enough that his life itself is given trying to gain what he can never enjoy.

You and I must work to provide for our families, and to fulfill our Calling in life. But there are many trees, full of bananas. It is our single minded, misplaced determination and improper attachment to unrewarding situations that keep us chained down, panicky, dissatisfied, and unable to move freely in life, as we are meant to live.

So, my friends, I encourage you... just let go of the damn banana. If it has chained you down, you are no longer free, and you are so tired of trying and trying to get what you want from an untenable situation: let it go. You may or may not find a different job. You may or may not start a new career. You may or may not take a leap of faith and finally start your own gig. But, by all means possible, detach from that which wearies you without reward. Let go of the banana. Slip free of the chains. Step back into the wild, where you get to choose for yourself how you will work and rest and love.

Carry nothing,

Christopher Bates

Portland, Oregon

DEDICATION

"We teach what we want to learn." — Rebecca Smith

This book is dedicated to you, sister.

ACKNOWLEDGEMENTS

Special thanks to these friends who directly influenced *Strategic Rest*:

Rod Brandt

Scott Jung

Rachel Hendrie

Bill Kieselhorst

Gary Marston

Rebecca Smith

Scott Soulages

Rob Vieira

I deeply appreciate your friendship, encouragement, and wise counsel.

ABOUT THE AUTHOR

Christopher lives in the beautiful Pacific Northwest and travels coast to coast and internationally to meet with consulting clients. He is a regular speaker at corporate events, and guest lecturer at colleges and universities. His client portfolio has a combined revenue in excess of $23B, and he is a recognized subject matter expert in CRM and sales and marketing business systems. He has billed over 25,000 consulting hours across private and public sector organizations, spent the equivalent of over one hundred straight days transiting the troposphere to visit clients, befriended hundreds of taxi drivers, survived an attempted mugging, and made a lot of mistakes - most of which he never intends to repeat.

For almost thirty years, Christopher Bates has helped organizations achieve sustainable productivity for significant growth. He combines proven productivity techniques with a deep understanding of how buyers think, to help companies tailor their approach to new target markets, increase revenues, and improve day to day performance.

Every client is different... but it is not uncommon for sales teams who work with Christopher to achieve double-digit growth in quarterly sales revenues in the years that follow his coaching.

In *PROFITABLE ROUTINES*, Christopher describes the five core habits in use by every successful team he has worked with. These five exercises, combined with a deep understanding of the Sales Maturity Model, allow sales teams to realign their sales efforts during market shifts, new product introductions, or shifts in leadership or focus.

Then, in *STRATEGIC REST*, Christopher takes an honest and candid look at the driven-ness built into corporate cultures, and walks us through a few key changes he has made over a period of years to clear his mind and keep his heart healthy, as he continues to invest in people and teams, year after year, managing tough projects and tight deadlines.